FIVE DEEP BREATHS

www.penguin.co.uk

FIVE DEEP BREATHS

The Power of Mindful Parenting

Dr Genevieve von Lob

BANTAM PRESS

LONDON · NEW YORK · TORONTO · SYDNEY · AUCKLAND

TRANSWORLD PUBLISHERS
61–63 Uxbridge Road, London W5 5SA
www.penguin.co.uk

Transworld is part of the Penguin Random House group of companies
whose addresses can be found at global.penguinrandomhouse.com

First published in Great Britain in 2017 by Bantam Press
an imprint of Transworld Publishers

A CIP catalogue record for this book
is available from the British Library.

ISBN 9780593077443

Typeset in 10.75/15.5pt Palatino LT Pro by Jouve (UK), Milton Keynes.
Printed and bound in Great Britain by Clays Ltd, Bungay, Suffolk.

Penguin Random House is committed to a sustainable
future for our business, our readers and our planet. This book
is made from Forest Stewardship Council® certified paper.

1 3 5 7 9 10 8 6 4 2

FIVE DEEP BREATHS

To all parents: past, present and future

Contents

Note to the reader

Welcome to *Five Deep Breaths*. I wrote this book to share the work I do with families with a wider audience, and I hope you will find it a valuable and inspiring companion on your journey as a parent.

For the sake of simplicity, I have tended to refer to parents as 'mums and dads'– though the word 'parent' can of course mean different things to different people. For some, a parent could be a grandparent, aunt, uncle, friend or stepparent, adoptive parent, foster carer or guardian. Some parents are in same-sex or transgender couples, and all come from different ethnic, religious and cultural backgrounds. Throughout *Five Deep Breaths*, the term 'parent' is intended to include all this diversity.

I am a chartered member of the British Psychological Society and the Health and Care Professions Council, and abide by their codes of ethics. I have not used any confidential material from my therapeutic work with clients in this book. All the 'case studies' featured in these pages are made-up composites designed to illustrate different themes I encounter in my work. All names are fictional, and any resemblance to real people is purely coincidental. I have also drawn on extensive interviews with parents who kindly agreed to discuss their experiences with me for the purposes of my research and gave me their consent to use the material anonymously in this book. Where reported speech appears in quote marks, it should be read as a paraphrasing to illustrate a general point, rather than a direct quotation.

It should be noted that the word 'mindfulness' can have different meanings in different contexts. In *Five Deep Breaths* I define 'mindfulness' in its broadest sense to mean the ability to step back and observe our thoughts and feelings. The 'mindfulness' exercises I have outlined are not drawn from any particular religious or contemplative tradition, but are based on the work I do in sessions with parents. There are various excellent books by psychologists and researchers who provide their own versions of mindfulness exercises, and I have listed a number of them in the References (page 233) and Resources (page 239). I have also provided references for the research from psychology or neuroscience I quote in the text.

Five Deep Breaths is not a substitute for professional support. I have included a list of helpful resources including organizations, websites and books on specific topics (page 239). Although I discuss mental health problems including anxiety, panic attacks, depression, ADHD and others, a detailed exploration of these and other medical conditions is beyond the scope of this book.

Some of the exercises I describe could potentially cause you to experience strong emotions. If at any time you feel you need more support, I would recommend you seek professional advice. Above all, I hope *Five Deep Breaths* will be a source of encouragement and reassurance that will endure long after you've turned the final page.

Dr Genevieve von Lob
London, April 2017
www.drvonlob.com / @drvonLob

Part I
You

Session
1

Ripping up the rule book

On the face of it, I might seem like the world's least qualified person to write a book for parents, having no children of my own and having grown up in a less than conventional family setting. I'd therefore like to take a moment to explain how I became a clinical psychologist working with hundreds of parents, teenagers and children from every conceivable type of background. Having spent years in both private practice and front-line NHS and local government mental health services, I've had the privilege of helping many mums and dads find their own answers to the dilemmas of modern parenting. Every day I'm awed and inspired by the courage and creativity of the parents and young people I meet, and I wrote this book to share something of the lessons we've learned together along the way.

My mother, Amanda, was a seventies wild child who in her late teens moved into a hippy commune in Norwich, where she scraped by singing in pubs and clubs. By the time I was born, she had grown into a headstrong twenty-two-year-old and I suspect my arrival was not entirely planned – I never knew the identity of my biological father. My mother later told me that having me spurred her to seek a clearer direction and on a whim she started singing lessons. To everyone's amazement, she beat intense competition to win a scholarship to train as an opera singer at the Royal Academy of Music in London. Determined to fulfil her ambition of becoming an international mezzo-soprano, she bundled me up along with a suitcase and moved us to a council flat in a tower block in Stepney Green. I had just turned two.

Though I could always sense my mother's love, our life together was a confusing juxtaposition of the grind of surviving in an almost penniless single-parent household on an East End estate and the glamorous world of opera, where I served as her shy sidekick – to the amusement, delight and sometimes consternation of her colleagues. Constantly dashing between rehearsals and classes, she would plonk me backstage, where a flamboyant cast of actors, singers and musicians arrayed in ball gowns or period costume would extravagantly fuss over me – an incongruous presence in the decidedly adult world of Mozart and Verdi. To my child's eyes, the immaculately made-up women looked like angels. Tiring of the attention, I would embark on lone expeditions deep into the hallowed corridors of the Academy – charting my path via the trill of a piano scale or the flourish of a clarinet. I dreaded returning to our tiny flat, where my mother was forced to accept a procession of lodgers to pay the bills. These strangers – as a child I called them 'the creatures' – would turn up unannounced, doss down on the sofa and help themselves to the meagre contents of our fridge.

My mother loved to share her beautiful voice and would warble scales as she did the housework. Her soaring mezzo tones were so powerful that I once saw her break a glass – causing her to collapse into giggles. But even her joyful octaves could not lift the oppressive atmosphere of the estate. I would regularly miss meals because she would run out of money, or she would be stuck at rehearsals as I was passed around among neighbours, and I was jealous of my mother's boyfriends, who often behaved as if I didn't exist. I can vividly remember the wash of relief I felt when, at the age of four, it was decided that I would temporarily return to Norwich to live with my grandparents while my mother completed her studies.

Despite our tough start, my mother's opera career began to blossom. She started doing television and theatre work and planned to set up her own travelling opera company so we could live together in Norwich. She put down a deposit on a beautiful Victorian house and took me to see my future bedroom – a wonderful converted attic. I couldn't wait to move in. The next morning, I was watching children's television when my grandparents did something unusual: they turned off the set and sat down with me on the sofa. They told me that my mother had been killed in a car accident while driving home to London the previous night. I was nine. My relatives were consumed by such grief that they found it impossible to talk to me about my feelings because they were struggling so hard to contain their own. I poured my pent-up emotion into an obsessive devotion to music, spending almost every spare minute of my childhood and teenage years learning to play the piano, dance, act and sing.

The next turning point came during my first year at university. I had been offered a place at a prestigious drama school, but my grandparents could not afford the fees and so I began a psychology degree instead – though I still harboured secret dreams of following in my mother's footsteps as a professional performer. One sweltering afternoon in exam season I was opening an antiquated sash window in the halls of residence when I slipped and fell. The glass shattered and I was rushed to hospital gushing blood from a deep gash in my right palm. My first thought was that I may never again play the piano.

While the injury was bad enough, the most painful part of the experience was the way the over-stretched medical staff seemed to look at me as dispassionately as if I were a specimen on a slab. It was only months later, when a physiotherapist showed a genuine curiosity about how I was feeling, that I felt anybody really cared. She spoke to me with such kindness that I broke down. Though our months of work together would save my hand from curling into a permanent claw, I was equally grateful for the interest she showed in my inner world. I realized that my future lay not in the performing arts, but in learning to extend to others the listening ear the physiotherapist had offered me. I embarked on the decade-long path of study needed to become a doctor of clinical psychology.

The doctoral training was unlike any other educational experience I had encountered. Our instructors encouraged us to work with our own childhood wounds to try to understand our present-day conflicts and troubling emotions. It was only by doing this work on ourselves that we could hope to be of use to anybody else. During the course, two more major life events occurred. When I was twenty-six, I lost my cousin Graeme – who was like a brother to me – to leukaemia. The following year I discovered the body of a flatmate – one of my best friends – who had died in the bath. Coupled with my losses in childhood, these experiences left me with a profound sense of unresolved grief – but they also served as a spur to the interior work that would later help me to reach others trapped in their own dark tunnels.

Throughout my journey, and my subsequent work with clients – from angry East End teenagers to stressed-out City executives – I have learned the value of exploring unwanted feelings. So often our dark moods or fears can seem like enemies; they can leave us feeling isolated and alone. But life has taught me that there is a way to work with these emotions and find the peace that lies just beyond them – if we can muster the courage and curiosity to keep going forward. As we progress, we may catch ourselves experiencing unexpected moments of calm or subtle joy that occur for no particular reason, like rays of sunlight that spill through a sudden break in the clouds. The goal is not to chase these revitalizing encounters, but to begin to build a new foundation for our lives in the pristine layer of peace that lies beneath the ever-changing kaleidoscope of our thoughts and feelings, whether we call them bad or good.

How 'mindfulness' can help parents

When it comes to raising children, there's no shortage of advice on offer. Friends, family, magazines, books and blogs – all are brimming with opinions on how to give your child the best chance of growing up happy, bright and successful. With so many options available, and so many contradictory theories, it's easy to start questioning whether you are making the right choices, or even secretly to wish there was some definitive manual on how to be a parent.

Five Deep Breaths is not that manual, because such a manual could never exist. Every child is unique, and the society they are growing up in is changing so fast that what may have worked yesterday might not be so relevant today. Some parents tell me they could never have imagined the weight of responsibility they would feel for somebody else's well-being until they experienced the joy of becoming parents themselves. It's all very well for experts to say that it's good for a child to undergo a few knocks and setbacks from time to time – but in reality, what parent wants to see their child suffer, even for a moment?

This book explores one simple truth: however great the pressures on modern mums and dads, there is always a way to lighten the burden – available right now, in this very moment, without the need to make any radical lifestyle changes or adopt a whole new parenting style. The core idea is 'mindfulness', which I define as the ability to hover above our thoughts and feelings so we no longer feel quite so overwhelmed. Whether it's dealing with day-to-day frustrations or more serious bouts of anxiety or depression, I have found that mindfulness is not some high-minded aspiration, but a sharp-edged tool anybody can learn to wield.

Let me be clear: *Five Deep Breaths* is not about striving to achieve some mysterious Zen-like state or finding a new reason to beat ourselves up when we lose it with our kids. I'm not going to be asking you to start getting up an hour earlier to sit cross-legged at sunrise, or to book your next summer holiday in an ashram or a monastery.

It's not about putting pressure on ourselves to be gracefully 'present' at all times, then feeling guilty when this inevitably proves impossible.

Five Deep Breaths is not about doing something extra, but about bringing more awareness into what we're already doing. With so much on our to-do lists, our minds are often racing: skipping ahead to the next task or over-thinking what's already in the past. This is a perfectly natural tendency, but the fact that everyone's mind is on overdrive doesn't make it any less exhausting.

Mindfulness offers a simple way to step back. This book will help you to remember to take the kind of little pauses to check in with yourself throughout the day that can make all the difference – taking the edge off stress and gradually helping us to connect with deeper dimensions of ourselves. We learn to meet each moment as utterly new and unique, and experience the natural openness of our minds and hearts. Old patterns start to lose their grip and we may discover that for all life's uncertainty and fragility, an undercurrent of peace and even joy may be much closer than we think.

As parents, we learn to become more comfortable with the fact that much of the time we're just doing our best to muddle through, and that's okay. Parenting inevitably involves periods of worry or doubt, and for anybody navigating choppier waters, I hope *Five Deep Breaths* will be both a reassuring companion and a source of practical guidance on how to tune in to your intuition and deepen your connection with your child.

Mindfulness has nothing to do with getting it 'right'. There's not a human being in history who has had the perfect upbringing, and any attempt to be a perfect parent is doomed to fail. There is no one-size-fits-all formula: everybody's experience as a mum or dad is different, and nobody will ever fully understand the unique set of challenges another person faces. Even within a family, siblings can have completely contrasting personalities and relate to their parents in different ways, while raising a child who has a disability or long-term illness can present its own set of dilemmas. Nevertheless, having seen how mindfulness has helped many parents from a wide range of backgrounds experience a greater sense of confidence, ease and flow, I wrote *Five Deep Breaths* with the goal of offering the essence of my one-on-one work to a broader audience.

In the following pages, I show how mindfulness can help us move from the kinds of feelings shown below on the left to those on the right:

I don't know if I'm doing the right thing.	*I'm handling myself better as a parent.*
I feel overwhelmed and I can't think straight.	*I'm more confident and I'm being kinder to myself.*
I'm not sure if I'm a good enough role model.	*I feel a greater sense of connection with my child.*
It's all my fault.	*I'm better at managing my children's moods – and my own.*
I'm always being judged.	*I'm learning to trust myself.*

Though mindfulness can undoubtedly deliver greater clarity, it is much more than a technique to help us complete to-do lists on time or strive to 'get ahead' in life. In essence, mindfulness is about opening the heart as well as quieting the mind – cultivating kindness and compassion for ourselves and others as well as greater mental clarity and calm. It certainly isn't about blissing out in a bubble and turning away from the many problems we're facing – whether they stem from the limitations of the school system, the gap between rich and poor or the violence being done to the natural world. I'm not offering a pill to make injustice more palatable or a distraction from the urgent task of challenging government incompetence or corporate greed – quite the contrary. As we begin to pay greater attention to what is going on in our own minds and bodies, we may discover a newfound sense of connection with the living web of our communities, nature and the planet as a whole. Mindfulness can help nurture precisely the kind of inner strength we will need if we are to take wise – perhaps radical – action on behalf of ourselves, our children – *all* children – and the generations to come.

While the practice of mindfulness has ancient roots, these are particularly exciting times for anybody choosing to explore it. For centuries, monks and sages have handed down techniques for establishing interior peace, but modern researchers equipped with powerful brain-imaging machines have begun to piece together theories as to why some forms of long-term meditation practice might be so beneficial. Neuroscience is also shedding new light on the ways young brains develop, and in *Five Deep Breaths* I have boiled down some of the most important insights into bite-size chunks designed to better equip a parent to respond to a younger child's meltdowns or a teenager's sullen withdrawal. I have also mined some of the most striking nuggets from the growing dossier of evidence on the benefits of mindfulness practice compiled by fellow psychologists. In my work with parents, I often find such research can provide an extra dose of motivation for giving the techniques a try and for sticking with practices that yield their richest rewards over time.

An invitation as you read

It's human nature to look outside ourselves for solutions. Parents often come to me when they are struggling and say, 'Just tell me what to do!' Or they may wish there was a 'magic pill' to solve their problems, even though they know at a rational level that this would be impossible. This book is not trying to be that 'magic pill' and it does not have any answers. What it does contain are tried-and-tested methods that I use to help parents develop their capacity to respond creatively and intuitively to any dilemma. The emphasis in this book is not on what you are *doing*, but in how you are *being* – a subject we explore in more depth in the next session. We begin to see that the endless striving to arrange circumstances to suit us never ends, but that we can find peace in the here and now. We may have the feeling we are seeing through fresh eyes, and gradually learn to look at our experiences from a new perspective.

Our culture has not traditionally placed much value on cultivating these kinds of qualities – the emphasis tends to be on striving for the sorts of success everybody else can admire: a great career; a wonderful relationship; model children. Yet it is the work we do on ourselves that has the power truly to transform our experience of being alive, investing our days with a sense of meaning and interconnectedness that can be profoundly reassuring, even in the darkest times. In my experience, these kinds of inner changes are inevitably reflected in the outer world of family, friends, relationships and career – though often in ways we might not expect. While there are many practical tips in these pages, the emphasis is on learning to trust the guidance of your head, heart and gut – the power centres where the wisdom of what I call our 'inner parent' resides. As we start to *feel* our thinking in this way, we may begin to find we develop a greater trust in ourselves and in our choices.

This journey is the work of a lifetime, but it takes only a single step to begin. For those embarking on this path for the first time, I hope this book will prove a reassuring guide, a 'pocket-therapist' that you will carry with you and return to again and again. For those who have already ventured forth, then I hope *Five Deep Breaths* will provide further encouragement and new vistas drawn from my experience working with many different kinds of families facing every imaginable problem.

Some sections may speak to you more clearly than others. There is no need to learn all the tools or practise all the exercises, but if you find a particular suggestion appeals, then I would encourage you to try it for a few days and see what happens. You may wish to underline or highlight sentences or bullet points that seem particularly relevant, or jot down notes in the journal section at the end of the book. If nothing else, glancing at the title *Five Deep Breaths* will serve as a cue to take a few seconds' pause – and this book will have done its job without leaving your shelf. There is no need to rush through these pages, and I would invite you to pause occasionally and reflect for a moment whenever you see the '✱' sign.

Towards a HEART-centred connection

In the last few years, there's been an explosion of interest in children's mental health. The media has increasingly featured stories quoting alarming statistics about the prevalence of anxiety, depression or self-harm among young people, as well as exam stress, potential dangers online and bullying. Once of concern primarily to parents, these problems are now being discussed by politicians, teachers and health professionals across Britain, and have even caught the attention of the Duke and Duchess of Cambridge, who are supporting the work of children's mental health charities and campaigning against stigma.

It's great to see this growing public acknowledgement of the need to support children who are struggling and to break down the remaining barriers around discussing our mental health. But we must not forget that children are like tuning forks: they will pick up on what the adults around them are going through, even if these adults are doing their best to keep their true feelings hidden. In my experience, children's 'symptoms' are often best understood not as evidence of an individual 'disorder' but as a reflection of the stresses swirling around them: at home, at school and in their communities. Few need to see a trained therapist, but they do need an authentic connection with someone who cares. As a mum or dad it can be painful to overhear a child saying, 'My parents just don't get me' or 'They never listen to my side of the story' – but with all the pressures on families, it can be hard to maintain the quality of relationship we might wish.

If we want to see happier kids, the first step is to help parents feel calmer, more confident and centred so they can provide the kind of compassionate, firm and intuitive leadership a child needs in order to feel nurtured and safe. I like to summarize the key components of this kind of connection with the acronym HEART:

- **H**umility. A willingness to accept that we are not perfect, but we simply do the best we can in the moment while aspiring to live by our values.

- **E**mpathy. Empathize with your child by remembering to take a moment to try to see the world through their eyes. Recognize that they have legitimate concerns and views.

- **A**uthenticity. In our busy lives as parents, stress can easily take over. The daily grind leaves us little space to explore how we truly feel. Authenticity is about having the courage to look at what's really going on for us. We all have ideas about how we're meant to feel and how we'd like to be seen by others. Practising authenticity is about being honest with ourselves, our children and the people closest to us.

- **R**espect. Respect is a two-way street, so respect yourself as an experienced adult whose well-being is just as important as that of your child. And show respect for your child by acknowledging that, while you may know more, they too have valuable lessons to teach.

- **T**rust. Trust yourself and your child, and believe that you can both handle life's ups and downs. Give them a chance to make mistakes in a safe, contained way that allows them to learn and grow.

Of course, all this can sound wonderful in theory, but the messy reality of modern parenting is rarely quite so simple. Nevertheless, children will have a much better chance of thriving if parents have access to tools that can help them provide the kind of calm and confident leadership they need. The rest of this book is about finding ways to embody these HEART-centred values – first in your relationship with yourself, and then with your child.

Dilemmas of the modern parent

Five Deep Breaths is not going to tell you what kind of parent you should be. My aim is to encourage and support you to look within – to be your own guru and listen to your own guidance. In my work, I'm struck by how many parents find it difficult to trust themselves. No matter what background they may have, or what particular issue they are facing, the core of the problem often consists of a lack of self-worth or a feeling of not being good enough. These are not the kinds of feelings we tend to discuss, but they have reached epidemic proportions in our society. So before we even begin to start working with mindfulness in my sessions, I find it often helps to share a broader perspective on the challenges of modern parenting to prove to worried mums and dads that they are far from alone.

We belong to a unique generation. We tend to be more open about our feelings than our parents or certainly our grandparents, and more aware of the influence our own upbringing may have had on the way we relate to our children. This greater level of self-awareness means that parents these days are often more willing to admit that they feel they're not getting it 'right' or that they're struggling with problems, such as anxiety or post-natal depression. Whether they reach out to friends or therapists, or share what they're going through online, parents are more open and more prepared to express their concerns than ever before. Blogs documenting the many difficulties of raising kids have reinforced this new culture of honesty around parenting and provided a valuable sense of solidarity for many mums and dads.

This greater self-awareness is a wonderful blessing in terms of helping us to understand ourselves and others. But it can also foster a gnawing fear that our children will fail to fulfil their potential or even resent us when they're older if we fail to conform to our model of an 'ideal' parent. Or we may start over-analysing – worrying that we might somehow be projecting an unaddressed conflict within ourselves on to our child. While the ease with which we can now read about the everyday struggles fellow parents are facing might be comforting, it can also feed niggling doubts about whether we're doing enough for our own children. In today's technology-driven and consumerist society, there seem to be so many choices to make. Which school? What should they be eating? How much time on the screen? What about social media? How about time for outdoor play and connecting with nature? What activities should they be doing? Are we setting the right limits? Are we spending enough time with them?

Answering these questions is hard enough, but in our

hyper-connected online world it's easy to feel that we're constantly being judged. It's as if we're addicted to comparing ourselves with others – and it's so easy to do as it's only a click away. Here are some of the themes that often surface in my conversations with parents:

- **Parenting as a competition.** It's natural for parents to want to do a good job, but I've noticed that many are increasingly telling me they feel as if they have been unwillingly thrust into an unspoken competition. Mums and dads often experience intense pressure to provide the same toys, phones, computers, activities or holidays as other parents because they don't want their own children to feel left out. Parents can also find themselves competing intensely to get their child into the 'right' school. It's very easy to think you're failing or not giving your kids enough opportunities, even though we all know deep down that forming a strong emotional connection with our child is more important in the long run than anything money can buy.

- **Feeling judged.** Working mums and dads can find themselves silently at odds with those who have given up their jobs to become full-time parents, injecting the same level of professionalism into making fancy-dress costumes or cupcakes as they did into their careers. Full-time mums or dads may, in turn, mourn the loss of their work status and feel that their partners undervalue the contribution they make. They may even feel resentful about dedicating these years entirely to raising a family.

- **Pressure-cooker classrooms.** Academic demands on children are constantly growing. One fourteen-year-old girl told me she was struggling to sleep at night because she was so anxious about the pressure placed on her by teachers – themselves under pressure to meet targets. Another anxious teen told me she was convinced she would end up homeless if she did not pass with flying colours. One child who was refusing to do his homework told me he'd been at school all day and needed a better 'work–life' balance – and he was only eight. Everyone wants their child to do well, but many parents are concerned that their children are being put under too much pressure by a 'factory-farm' school system where assessments are being conducted at ever younger ages. Academic research has shown that play is essential for healthy brain development, but recreation is increasingly being squeezed out of timetables.

● **Time famine.** For many parents, balancing the competing demands of the workplace, parenthood and perhaps caring for their own older parents can seem like an impossible task. Days can turn into a struggle just to keep your head above water and you may feel constantly stretched to the limit.

● **Criticism – from self and others.** Sometimes our parents, friends or relatives may offer well-intentioned advice, but usually our harshest judge is ourself. All of us have inherited a template – perhaps without realizing it – of what an 'ideal' family should look like. We may find ourselves struggling to live up to impossible goals, or driven to over-compensate for what we perceive as our own parents' failings. Or we may fear that people will interpret our attempts to set appropriate limits as a sign of emotional coldness or a controlling personality, and that they will perhaps conclude that we don't really love our child.

● **Digital dilemmas.** Social media is magnifying peer pressure – for children and their parents. Young girls pout for selfies, teenagers constantly compare their looks with those of their peers or media stars, and old-fashioned bullying has migrated into cyberspace. Many mums and dads are also concerned about what kind of images their children may be exposed to online, what they're reading and who they may be communicating with. Parents feel the pressure too – bombarded by endless pictures posted by other mums or dads, or stories of celebrities who seem to have the perfect family, the perfect marriage, the perfect body and the perfect life.

- **Building resilience.** We all know that children need opportunities to learn that it's okay to make mistakes or experience failure. Only by working through challenges and overcoming setbacks can they develop the resilience they will need to navigate the inevitable ups and downs of adult life. But it can be hard to strike a balance between letting your child explore and take risks and the discomfort you may feel when they struggle. How do we know what's right?

- **A drought of self-compassion.** In our society, we're all much too hard on ourselves. We're brought up to believe that 'success' is all-important, whether it's at school, in our jobs, in our relationships and especially as parents. We can spend a great deal of energy pushing ourselves – and then beating ourselves up when things don't work out as planned. This harsh attitude can easily spill over into our attempts to be a little calmer. When we try mindfulness for the first time and notice how busy our minds are, we immediately conclude that we've 'failed' and end up feeling worse than when we started. Similarly, many of us hold ourselves to impossible standards as parents and find it very difficult to accept that being 'good enough' is okay.

The stakes have never been higher – not just for parents, but for society as a whole. There can be no more important task than providing a firm foundation for the next generation to grow into independent, well-balanced and resourceful adults brimming with inspiration for building a better world. Yet with all these dilemmas to face, and all the conflicting advice, it's easy to feel that as a parent, you just can't win.

Five deep breaths

Sometimes when a mum or dad comes to see me, they know they feel bad, but they don't know why. They often judge themselves harshly for feeling this way because they are aware of other parents who seem to be cheerfully coping with much more difficult problems. They say things like, 'Quite honestly, I had a great childhood – I had wonderful parents,

I went to a nice school – generally things have been good. So why don't I feel happy? Why do I feel like such a complete failure?'

Everyone's life is complex and it's not always obvious where the stress is coming from. As humans, we have a wide range of ways of responding to difficulties, but there are a number of common patterns that can play out when we feel that something is wrong in our lives:

- **Worry.** We constantly think about a problem or imagine worst-case scenarios. We believe at some level that it's good to expect the worst, even though the stress of so much worrying wears us down.

- **Self-blame.** We put pressure on ourselves by imagining that we should be doing 'better' in our lives, or that things have gone wrong in some way and that we are responsible. We imagine that *if only* we had acted differently, then everything would be okay.

- **Denial.** We refuse to look at a problem and pretend to ourselves that everything is fine, even when we know deep down that things aren't quite right and we need to address difficult issues.

- **Feeling empty.** Many of us are not content with where we are in our lives and believe that our circumstances have to change in order for us to feel better. We spend much of our energy chasing after the next relationship, a new job, more money, special possessions, social status or the next holiday. We might feel good when we get what we want, but soon the craving for more returns.

- **Overdoing it.** Whether it's working too hard, drinking or eating too much, or numbing ourselves with shopping, television or digital distractions, it's easy to find ways to run from our feelings. Of course, these activities can be very enjoyable in moderation – but they can become harmful if they are being used as a mask to hide underlying unease.

We will be exploring a wide range of ways to step out of these kinds of patterns throughout this book, but the simplest and most effective starting point is something so familiar we barely even notice it – our breath.

For many people, the idea that an act as simple as paying a little more attention to the way we inhale and exhale air may yield very tangible results sounds almost too good to be true. 'You're telling me to breathe?' was the irritated response from one dad. 'I do that anyway.' People tend to be more eager to discuss their very real problems, rather than to devote precious time to acquainting themselves with an activity that seems to happen perfectly well all by itself.

Nevertheless, bringing greater awareness into the way we breathe is perhaps the single most powerful tool for rapidly gaining greater clarity and self-awareness. The breath is the link between our body and mind, and science is very clear about why paying more attention to it can be so helpful.

Picture a car speeding down a motorway at 100 mph: that's the build-up of stress. Taking slow, deep breaths engages something called the Vagus nerve, which acts like a brake. This huge nerve connects our brain with our heart and other major organs before meandering all the way down into the depths of our gut. (The word *vagus* in Latin means 'wandering' – the word 'vagabond' has the same root.)

When we breathe deeply, the Vagus nerve has a soothing effect: our heart rate slows, our blood pressure falls and we reduce production of the stress hormone cortisol. We also strengthen the pathways in the brain associated with a sense of calm. The next time you feel stressed, take five deep breaths and feel your entire body soften and your frazzled feelings start to fade. (Recent studies have shown that the Vagus nerve also responds to human connection and physical touch, so a hug works too.)

Try It: Mindful breathing

Notice how you are breathing. Bringing your attention to your breath for even ten seconds has a noticeably calming effect on the body. Is it shallow or deep? Are you holding your breath, tightening your stomach or hunching your shoulders?

● Inhale deeply through the nose for a count of five, making sure that the tummy expands. It can help to imagine it filling up with air like a balloon. There's no need to strain. If it feels unnatural to breathe into the belly, then simply breathe as deeply as you can into your chest.

● Hold the breath for a count of five. If the mind wanders, gently come back to the breath – without judging yourself for losing focus.

● Then exhale completely through the mouth. Really feel like you're letting it all go. The out-breath should take a little longer than the in-breath.

● It can be helpful to place your hands on your tummy so that you can really feel the expansion and contraction as you breathe in and out.

Repeat this several times until you are feeling a little more relaxed.

Breathe more deeply, live more deeply

The beauty of this practice is that it's easy to make it part of your daily life – it's simply a question of bringing more attention to what you are already doing all the time. I find many parents benefit from building little reminders into their day to take five deep breaths until it becomes a habit. For example:

- A bedside reminder to start the day with five deep breaths.

- Take a breath every time you find yourself waiting for the kids in the morning/before serving dinner/before putting them to bed.

- Taking slow breaths until a red traffic light changes to green.

- When you're waiting for the kettle to boil.

- Before you reply to a text message or email.

- There are also apps that you can program to remind you to breathe (see page 254 for some suggestions).

There's no great mystery to this exercise – it's just a way of tapping into our in-built relaxation system. Change doesn't happen overnight, but as you familiarize yourself with your breath, you will discover an anchor-line that you can always use to return to the present, no matter how much your mind wants to rake over the past or worry about what might happen in the future. By learning to breathe more deeply, we learn to live more deeply in the only place and time there is: the here and now.

*

The five key points
Ripping up the rule book

● Today's parents face unique challenges: you're not alone.

● There's no rule book for parenting: learn to trust yourself.

● A HEART-centred connection will last for a lifetime.

● Use this book as a pocket-therapist to support your journey.

● In any situation, taking five deep breaths is a good place to start.

Session 2

The 'frenemy' within

It's 6:23 a.m. You've just managed to roll out of bed and stumble bleary-eyed into the kitchen in search of a coffee, only to find your six-year-old bouncing with energy and determined to play. She has her own ideas about what an enjoyable start to the day looks like – and it doesn't involve getting dressed for school. She's much more interested in rebuilding the den she made out of cushions in the living room last night. Meanwhile, your eight-year-old is in his room, slumped into his pillows and no doubt already immersed in Minecraft on the iPad, while your thirteen-year-old still hasn't woken up. You have only one goal: to get all three dressed and fed and out the door with a fighting chance of making it to school on time, preferably with their teeth brushed and their shoes laced. 'Muuuum,' your six-year-old says, suddenly bored of her den-reconstruction project. 'I know you won't say "yes" – but can I watch TV?'

It's only the hundredth time you've had this conversation – and the outcome will depend purely on how exhausted you're feeling. In this case, you decide to put your foot down. Your six-year-old scrunches up her face and says, 'I don't even *like* you,' before storming off to her room, where you can be pretty certain she won't be getting ready. By this point, your thirteen-year-old has dragged himself out of bed and is asking if you've got his gym kit ready and found his missing homework. As you serve breakfast, all three siblings start arguing with each other. Your six-year-old spills her juice, runs away from the table and starts chasing the dog.

An edge creeps into your voice as you tell her as calmly as possible to get her shoes on, but she looks you straight in the eye, then turns and runs away again. Before you can help it, you've lost your temper and you're screaming at all three of them, 'We've got ten minutes. Can we please all just get a *move on!*' Whatever you might have heard about 'mindfulness', you're pretty sure that it doesn't involve screeching at the top of your voice then spending your journey to work beating yourself up for losing your temper. So, what exactly *is* mindfulness? And how can it help?

'Being' versus 'doing'

The origins of our present-day interest in mindfulness can be traced back to the 1950s and 60s, when growing numbers of Westerners began to explore Eastern wisdom traditions. In more recent times, there has been an explosion of research into the potential for mindfulness to help us cope with the stresses of modern living. Schools, companies and many other institutions are adopting mindfulness programmes – and the British parliament has even produced a report on its benefits.

With so many people talking about it, it's not surprising there's a lot of confusion over what mindfulness is all about. But first, let's be clear on what it isn't:

● It doesn't mean you are expected to attain a permanent state of calm where even the stress of the morning routine doesn't bother you any more.

● Mindfulness does not mean trying to stop thinking. It doesn't mean trying to make your mind go blank, or emptying your head like a bucket.

- It doesn't have to involve long periods sitting on a cushion or lighting joss sticks.

- It's not a means of running away from problems or indulging in wishful thinking.

- In mindfulness, there is nothing to 'get right' and you cannot fail. It's always there waiting for you to pick up again in a new moment.

For most of our waking hours, we're focused on getting things done. We have our big life goals in terms of family and career, and we have our daily to-do lists – on paper, on our phones and in our heads. With all the pressures on modern families, these lists never seem to end. We can easily find ourselves skipping from one task to the next, planning and problem-solving without ever really giving our full attention to what we're doing in the here and now. We may feel that our busy minds are making us productive – but in fact we're a bundle of distractions.

Although there are times when we have to rely on autopilot just to get us through the day, we can pay a high price if we live like this all the time. We can end up drained by the feeling that there's never enough time, and frustrated when we don't tick off all our tasks. We may miss out on the everyday richness in our lives because we're just too distracted to notice the simple things happening right in front of us – like our child's smile or the way sunlight is filtering through the leaves outside our window. The people around us lose out too because, though we may be there in body, they can sense that our minds are elsewhere.

Mindfulness offers an alternative. We can switch from what the meditation teacher Jon Kabat-Zinn calls 'doing mode' into 'being mode'. We don't have to change *what* we're doing, rather *how* we're doing it. In 'being mode' we bring our attention fully into the present moment. We choose to focus on what we're doing, rather than allowing our mind to run ten steps ahead. Some teachers compare the mind to a monkey scampering through the trees and liken mindfulness to teaching the monkey to sit still on a mat. In essence, we learn to do one thing at a time, giving each moment our full attention, and learning to respond rather than react.

As we progress, we begin to develop a new relationship with our thoughts and feelings. We learn to observe what's going on inside us rather than being swept away. We cultivate the ability to take a step back when we're starting to feel overwhelmed and learn instead to take a moment to become more aware of what we're thinking and feeling. Imagine climbing out of a fast-flowing river and sitting on the bank, peacefully watching thoughts flow past like leaves swirling in the current.

Even if we notice we're having thoughts or feelings we don't like, we resist the impulse to push them away and instead begin to explore them with an attitude of curiosity, openness and kindness towards ourselves. This might seem difficult, or even impossible, at first – but the more we practise this softer, non-judgemental attitude, the easier it becomes. Rather than running as fast as we can, we learn that slowing down gives us options. We realize we don't have to get so caught up in the thoughts and feelings that bring us down, and that we can always make a choice about how we respond to each new situation.

Mindfulness doesn't require busy parents to set aside any of their precious time. It simply requires that we inhabit our moments more fully. In 'being mode' we can still get things done. In fact, we may find our days unfold more smoothly as we are less distracted and more alert. We can learn so much from our young children, who can teach us what it is to live more fully in the present. And as we experience 'being mode' more often, we may find we start to see things in a new light – our children, our partner, and ourselves.

Julie: Switching into 'being mode'

'I'm really noticing a difference if I can just remember to be in the here and now a bit more often, and not always be thinking about everything I have to do. I know when Ben comes in from school I've got a million things on my mind – I'm doing the cooking but I'm thinking about when I'm going to get a chance to take the cat to the vet. I go through the motions of asking Ben how his day went – but I miss half of what he's actually saying because my mind's racing ahead. I'll ask him about how his Maths test went over dinner and he'll look all crestfallen and say, "I already told you earlier."

'By focusing on one thing at a time, I'm getting better at noticing when I'm getting distracted. I try not to get annoyed with myself and try to take a few deep breaths to keep myself anchored in the present. When Ben comes in I try to focus more on him and what he's saying. I've found that even thirty seconds of being fully there with him is much better than just saying, "That's nice, love," and carrying on with other things. It doesn't matter if I don't have time for a long chat – we can always pick up on things later – but just those few moments of real connection make a big difference to us both.'

Filling in gaps

We've all had the experience of making a snap judgement about a situation or person, only to discover that our first impressions were wide of the mark. I saw this most clearly myself some years ago, when I had just qualified as a clinical psychologist. I was obsessing over an ambiguous text from a boyfriend, coming up with all kinds of interpretations of what he might mean. My friend Kirsty turned to me in exasperation and said, 'You're filling in gaps.' And of course she was right. My mind had made up a story that I believed without question – but was it even true? I hadn't stopped to think. When we begin to examine our thoughts more closely, it can be quite a shock to realize how often our minds fill in gaps in this way, often worrying about things which may never happen, or inventing explanations that we later recognize don't fit the facts.

Of course, this is not to deny that problems do exist. It's completely normal for parents to worry, particularly when there are real concerns about their child. But worrying about what might happen in the future can easily take us over and make it harder to deal with the challenges we're actually facing in the here and now. We may think our worrying is helpful, but in reality it's mostly just draining us. Our own mind is behaving like a 'frenemy' living in our head.

Here's an example of what I mean. Let's imagine the following scenario. Say you receive a voicemail from your son's school asking you to call his head of year, but they don't say what it's about. Suddenly the gap-filling begins: 'What's happened to my son? Has he done something wrong? Is he in trouble? Has he forgotten to do his homework again?' Before you know it, the mind has created a worst-case scenario and you're frantic with worry. Ten minutes later, you get hold of the school and find out that all they wanted was to follow up on an innocent query related to a school trip. All the worry was caused by your mind going into overdrive. How often do we find ourselves caught in stories about ourselves or others that may not be true?

The more I worked with parents, the more I came to see that 'filling in gaps' is a universal problem. It's so automatic that we don't even notice our minds are doing it, constantly creating stories that often make us feel worse. Our minds are obviously wonderful tools – but they can easily lead us astray. Though the problems faced by families are very real, we often have more options at our disposal than we realize. Mindfulness helps us to perceive our mental chatter for what it is: a stream of thinking that often misleads us, behaving more like a 'frenemy' than a helpful ally.

A new relationship with the 'frenemy'

Our minds are far more powerful than we often realize. Every second of the day, we're interpreting what is happening around us based on our past experiences, our upbringing, our personality and our beliefs. The way our minds filter what's happening makes all the difference between whether we often feel stressed and anxious or whether we're more able to accept life as it comes. Our habitual way of seeing the world is so familiar that we rarely pause to question how helpful it is.

When I work with parents, I often try a little experiment. I ask them to imagine that they are hooked up to a machine that records every single one of their thoughts over twenty-four hours. It would be like having a sort of digital PA who produces a written transcript of everything that's gone through your head. For example, an excerpt from the transcript might look something like this:

> 'I can't believe I shouted at my kids again this morning. I bet no one else's kids have to hear their mother yelling at them before breakfast! I'm a bad mum – I'm failing my children. I really just need a bit of space – but there isn't time. I should get up an hour earlier – that would help me be more on top of everything. But I'm too tired to get up that early. I need to do better, be more organized and in control . . .'

I then ask the parent to consider:

- How many thoughts does their twenty-four-hour transcript contain?

- How many of these thoughts were actually helpful?

- How many of these thoughts were critical of *you*?

The point is not to come up with precise answers, but to use these questions to start to appreciate just how busy our minds can get. It can be quite a surprise to realize what a chatterbox we have for company, and how often it decides to subject us to a barrage of criticism or blame.

Some mums and dads break into a smile or even laugh out loud when they see this clearly. So much of the time, our thoughts are going around in circles, distracting us from what we're doing or putting a negative spin on things. It's no wonder so many of us feel worn-out, edgy and stressed.

The stream never stops. You could take a thirty-second section of the transcript from virtually any time of the day and the chances are that your mind would be feeding you a similar diet of thoughts – worrying about the to-do list, going over things that happened in the past or imagining what could go wrong in the future. We believe that we think our thoughts, but often our thoughts seem to be thinking us. What if we paused to look more closely? As we start to pay more attention, we may begin to understand that – at the deepest level – we are the *observer* of our mind, and not the stream of opinions, judgements and speculation it constantly pours forth.

The spiritual teacher Eckhart Tolle suggests another helpful exercise for stepping back from the stream of our habitual thinking in his excellent book *The Power of Now.* Imagine for a moment that you are a cat, waiting by a mousehole. Can you stay alert without thinking any thought at all? Or does a thought suddenly appear? What does the thought say? Where did it even come from? Does it deserve to be taken seriously? Is it even true?

*

Tricks of the mind

Our negative patterns of thinking can be so familiar that we often assume that they are a fundamental part of who we are. On closer inspection, we may start to see them more as habits, much like biting our nails or smoking. Of course, habits are not always easy to break – but we can find ways to work with them.

To help us do this, pioneering researchers including Dr Aaron Beck and Dr David Burns have explored the way we are prone to falling into what psychologists call 'thinking traps' – typical ways in which our minds lose perspective and make a situation seem worse than it actually is. You may wish to ask yourself if any of the below seem familiar:

Common Thinking Traps

- **Black-and-white thinking.** No shades of grey: *'I'm the worst parent in the world. It's the one thing I should be able to do, and I can't. If I'm not perfect as a parent, I'm a complete failure.'*

- **Catastrophizing.** Assuming the worst possible outcome: *'That's it, I lost it again. I have messed up my child for ever. They will hate me and have to spend the rest of their life in therapy – and they'll put all the blame on me.'*

- **Mind-reading.** Jumping to conclusions about what others are thinking, without any evidence: *'She's definitely judging me for deciding to send my children to private school.'*

- **'Should' statements.** Telling yourself how you 'should' or 'must' act: *'I've only got one child, but other parents with much bigger families are breezing through. I should be able to cope.'*

- **Focusing on negatives.** Dwelling on problems and downplaying positives: *'It doesn't matter that I've been calmer lately and things seem to be on a more even keel. The fact I lost it in the supermarket in front of everyone has ruined everything.'*

- **Disqualifying positives.** We discount the good things in our life and dismiss possibilities for improvement with: *'Yes, but . . .'*

- **Self-labelling.** Habitually calling ourselves names: *'I'm such an idiot. I'm a loser.' 'I'm so weak.' 'I'm such a mean dad.'*

Continued . . .

> ● **Over-generalizing.** One bad thing happens and we say: *'My kids won't stop squabbling today: everything always goes wrong for me as a parent.'*

The 'frenemy' is a master story-teller

As we begin to notice how much of the time our mind is going over the same old ground, we may discover that its stories follow familiar themes – a little like the scripts of old movies we've seen a thousand times. Once we start to recognize them for what they are – just stories – their power over us begins to weaken. We begin to realize we don't need to believe everything our mind tells us. Here are some of the movie scripts I typically encounter with parents:

The 'guilt' script

This is a big one: so many parents tell me they are worried that they have failed their child in some way because of what they did or did not do. Every parent experiences a degree of guilt at some point in their life – it's a sign that you care about doing the best you can, and it can encourage you to make positive changes. But guilt becomes a problem when it starts to take over your life and you feel there's no way out. Here are some examples of the 'guilt script' in action:

> *'I feel terrible about sending my son to nursery because I had to go back to work. I know I spoil him to make it up to him, and that makes me feel even more guilty.'*

> *'I get impatient with my daughter's constant questions and that makes me feel like a horrible parent.'*

> *'I feel guilty for saying that I'm bored of taking my daughter to the swings for the ten millionth time when there are people who can't have children.'*

'I feel guilty that I don't seem to be able to remain calm and composed and be a good role model for my son.'

'I feel guilty that I'm always arguing with my partner in front of the kids.'

'She's inherited all my anxiety and over-sensitivity.'

'I feel guilty for not feeling more gratitude when there are so many other families who are much worse off than us.'

'I feel guilty that I can't afford to send my daughters to dance lessons. They're missing out and it's my fault.'

'I feel terrible about the stress my youngest son faced as a baby: it was a difficult birth and I had post-natal depression. My other kids got a much more chilled-out mum.'

'I let them watch too much TV and don't play with them enough.'

'I don't feel particularly guilty when I leave them to go out and have some "me time", so I end up feeling guilty about not feeling guilty.'

'I feel guilty that their dad and I are not together any more.'

'I wish I'd been able to give each of my children more individual attention.'

'I experience guilt over the fact that I don't seem to be able to just be in the here and now and savour every moment I have with my children. I know these precious years are rushing by, and one day I will look back and wish I had enjoyed them more.'

Kelly: Too guilty for 'me time'

'My husband gave me a spa day for my birthday last summer but I haven't used it yet. It feels frivolous to spend a whole day away from the children faffing around in a dressing gown. But it would be really good for me to go – I really need some "me time", to moan with friends or just get a little bit of head space. I don't know why I feel guilty. I don't know why I can't give myself permission to take a little time away. Since I do so much of the parenting, it's as if I've entered the mindset that I always have to do it all – and I feel guilty if anyone else does anything. Handing over control is hard. I am a control freak. I always have been. I even feel guilty if my mum picks up the kids for me – I worry: will they behave? It's hard to let go.'

The 'being judged' script

It's very common for parents to feel they're being judged by other parents, or by their own parents and in-laws, who are convinced they know the 'right' way to raise children. Of course, we can all be a little judgy at times – it's part of human nature – and most of us are our own harshest critic. However, if you're feeling under attack from others, bear in mind that the opinions of those who would pass judgement reveal a lot more about them than they do about you. Here are some examples of the 'being judged' script in action:

'I'm scared my child's birthday party won't measure up.'

'I'm a working mum and I'm sure other parents think I don't spend enough time with my children.'

'I'm a stay-at-home mum and I feel like people see me as a drudge and a second-class citizen.'

'I thought that as a woman I knew what it was to be judged, but I realized I didn't really know what that meant until I became a mum. It seems like everyone has an opinion on how best to raise your child!'

'My mother's always criticizing the way I discipline my kids – she says I'm too soft and I let them spend too much time on the iPad or in front of the TV.'

'Now I'm a parent, I will never judge another parent again – you don't know what they've had to deal with all day.'

Karen: 'I know I shouldn't compare myself'

'I'm so scared of being judged that my stress levels are through the roof and everything has to be "just right". We've just been on a family holiday to Spain, which should have been a relaxing break, but I was so het up about making everything perfect and trying to make sure that everyone else had a good time that I couldn't relax and enjoy the holiday. I was on edge the whole time and kept bursting into tears. I know I shouldn't, but I can't stop judging myself harshly compared with the other mums at Mark's school. I had some of them round for dinner a few weeks ago and I nearly had a panic attack trying to make sure everything was absolutely perfect. I found it all very exhausting. I wish I could just learn to stop worrying about what other people think.'

The 'what if' script

Worry is perhaps the commonest script of all. It's a given that as a parent you're going to worry more – whether you experience nagging 'what if' thoughts or find yourself constantly contemplating worst-case scenarios. Often the most caring people worry the most. However, worrying can be exhausting and counter-productive when it goes round in endless circles without leading to constructive action:

'What if my son's under too much pressure at school?'

'I'm worried about whether my kids are going to turn out okay.'

'What if my son's spending too much time on his Xbox?'

'I worry my daughter's got into the wrong crowd.'

'Since we've had kids our relationship's not been the same.'

'What if we've chosen the wrong school?'

'I'm worried my teenage son is unable to take responsibility for basic things like his homework and household chores.'

'What if my kids only remember the stressful times, even though I've tried my best to make it up to them?'

Dave: 'I'm worried about going back to work full-time'

'I find it hard to sleep at night because I'm not sure I made the right decision to go back to work full-time. Maybe it will affect my bond with Kayleigh, my seven-year-old, if I'm not at home with the family so much? But we really need the money, and I need a different focus and the adult company.'

Flipping the script

As we become more familiar with our 'frenemy's' favourite movie scripts, a new question arises: now what?

The first thing to remember is that we can't just get rid of our 'negative' thoughts – and fighting them just makes them worse. It's an old psychologist's cliché to point out that if I say, 'Don't think of a pink elephant,' then one will inevitably pop into your mind's eye. That's just the way the brain works. Trying to stop your thoughts is about as futile as trying to stop waves on the ocean with a giant pane of glass. The good news is that even noticing that you are replaying an old script will make it easier to start to look at things in a more resourceful way. Some parents find the following exercises useful:

- **Write the storyline down.** When I was going through a phase of high anxiety a few years ago, I found it very helpful to write the content of my worry on my smartphone. For example: 'I am feeling like I'm wasting my life and always seem to be behind on everything.' Some parents use a diary or notebook to catalogue their worries, and this can be a surprisingly effective way to weaken their intensity (so much so that there are entire schools of psychotherapy based on writing). You may wish to use the journal at the back of this book (page 259).

- **Visualize releasing the story.** Some parents imagine pinning their worries, guilt script or feelings of being judged on to a passing cloud, placing them gently on a leaf floating by on a stream or launching them to a distant star. You might also experiment with visualizing negative feelings as train passengers and watch them step off your carriage before you continue with your journey. Or you could try releasing your 'frenemy' and all the angst it causes.

- **Turn down the volume.** Just as we can turn down the volume on a news channel pumping out depressing stories that we can't immediately do anything about, we can make a conscious choice to turn down the volume on our worries. It can be helpful to visualize turning down a radio to reduce the intensity of negative thoughts – and then adjust the dial to a station with more positive messages.

*

Working with worry

There's a reason why thinking positively can seem so difficult. Our brains have evolved to focus on potential threats; if they hadn't then our ancestors wouldn't have lasted very long. Worrying about being attacked by wild animals or running out of food – rather than stopping to smell the flowers or appreciate the sunset – is what has kept our species alive. We've inherited the same negative bias. Given the amount of responsibility parents have and the number of tasks they're facing each day, worry is inevitable. As many parents tell me, 'Worrying is what helps me to be caring and responsible and keep my family safe. If I don't worry, who will?'

Worry is good if it really is helping us to solve problems or take helpful action. The problems start when our worry gets so out of hand that it begins to consume our day-to-day lives and leave us feeling anxious and drained. We can find ourselves covering the same ground over and over again, without really getting anywhere. It's like following well-worn tracks on a ski slope: we fall into the same old grooves without realizing there may be another path we can take. There's a big difference between sitting down to solve a problem and going round and round in circles worrying about all the bad things that could happen that you can't control. Many of us worry that we can't seem to stop worrying. It's easy to start feeling helpless.

In mindfulness, the goal is not to fight our thoughts and feelings, but gradually to change our relationship with them. We begin to examine whether a particular pattern of thought is serving us and whether there might be other perspectives we can consider. Of course, this isn't always easy – and the mind loves nothing more than to tell us that we can't step back from our thoughts, and that we might as well give up trying. The trick is to start to see these thoughts as just another unhelpful script.

When we find ourselves in the grip of worries, it can help to reflect on the following questions:

- Is this a pressing problem or a hypothetical 'what if' issue?

- Is there something I can do about this right now?

- Does it make more sense to plan to tackle this in the future?

These questions can help us start to draw a clearer distinction between the constructive process of carefully and calmly thinking through a problem, and the 'frenemy's' tendency to dwell on worst-case scenarios or point an accusing finger of self-blame.

'Dandelion' thoughts

Some thoughts can be a little like dandelions – however many times you think you've plucked them they keep growing back. In such cases, it can be helpful to take a systematic, step-by-step approach to learning to relate to them differently. The following 'thought-labelling' exercise is adapted from *The Happiness Trap* by Dr Russ Harris, one of the leading proponents of a form of psychotherapy called Acceptance and Commitment Therapy (ACT), which was founded by Drs Steven Hayes, Kirk Strosahl and Kelly Wilson:

Try It: Labelling thoughts

The first step is to identify a painful, repetitive thought that causes a feeling of distress. It might be something like: *'I am a bad parent'*, *'I am an unfit parent'* or *'I am a failure as a parent.'*

● Once you have identified the thought, think silently to yourself:

'I am not a good enough parent' (or whatever your thought is).

● Then think:

'I am having a thought that *I am not a good enough parent'* (or insert your thought here).

Continued . . .

Notice what that feels like, and where any feeling occurs in your body.

● Then think:

'I am noticing that I am having the thought that *I am not a good enough parent'* (or insert your thought here).

Again, notice how this new thought feels, and where any feeling occurs in your body.

● How do you feel after following these steps? Often parents find that they feel a bit more removed from their uncomfortable feeling, and they start to recognize that their thought is *just* a thought.

Conclude this exercise by expressing appreciation for your mind and all the wonderful things it can do – even if you do not always choose to follow the particular train of thought it's generating. You can say to yourself: *'Thank you, mind, but today I am choosing not to go down that road/believe that story/follow that script.'*

*

Jennifer: 'I'm learning to catch my thoughts'

'The worst times are at bedtime and in the mornings. Sometimes Liam seems okay, but more and more he doesn't seem to listen to anything I say. He always seems to be playing games on his phone and if I try to set limits or give him instructions he says really horrible things to me. I almost can't believe it's coming from the mouth of a nine-year-old, especially my own son. I try to get him to do his homework, but he

refuses – and I find myself losing my temper. Then I feel terrible afterwards and worry that I'm turning into one of those awful "shouty" mums. Nothing could have prepared me for how stressful being a mum is – my mind's just constantly on overdrive. I have a million thoughts a day – it's so crazy and manic. I feel like I'm going insane sometimes. I keep bursting into tears. I can't stop worrying and thinking the worst.'

At first, Jennifer cries as she tells her story, feeling frustrated and ashamed. I work with her to help her to become more aware of what she's thinking. When she's starting to feel upset, she silently asks, *'What's going on in my mind right now?'*

Jennifer gradually starts to notice how often she seeks to push away her difficult thoughts and feelings by keeping constantly busy or drinking one or two extra glasses of wine. She identifies the following themes: *'I've ruined everything. I'm a bad mum. Everyone's better than me.'*

As Jennifer learns to step back from her busy mind, she starts to catch herself when an old 'script' has begun to play. She makes a note of her thoughts on her phone, which helps her to see them more objectively. She also learns to express appreciation for her mind, which helps her to avoid being too harsh on herself.

Jennifer makes a point of taking five deep breaths – during her commute, at the office, when she's cooking and while she's lying in bed at night. She likes to silently say the word 'calm' as she's breathing out. She starts to notice when she's going around in circles, and gets better at remembering to pause and ask, *'Is this something I can do anything about right now? Are these thoughts taking me anywhere?'*

Gradually, Jennifer starts to feel calmer and finds that her negative thoughts don't have quite so much power. She is able

Continued . . .

to see that her old 'scripts' are just stories – not necessarily facts. Her son senses the shift and over time their relationship improves.

'I'm able to say, "Ah, okay – I'm getting really angry here",' Jennifer says. *'I ask myself, "Can I take a few deep breaths before I say or do anything I might regret?" I'm recognizing I've got more options than I realize. I don't have to act so impulsively, or to take my mind quite so seriously.'*

Coming to your senses

The beauty of mindfulness is that you can take a simple step to start cultivating it immediately – and feel the difference it makes. There are many different techniques, but the simplest one I tend to use with parents is developing a natural ability we are all born with but sometimes forget to use: the capacity to focus our attention more fully on what's going on around us.

Many people find the easiest way to do this is simply to bring their attention back to their in-breath – the anchor-line to the present moment. Let's try it now. Be with your breath: feel the feeling of the air on your nostrils, the rise and fall of your chest and abdomen. Notice your mind's tendency immediately to begin to wander and start coming up with comments or analysis. Try to refrain from judging this tendency – it's just your mind being your mind. With each new moment, bring your attention gently back to your breath, and then see how you feel. You can try a similar technique by focusing more fully on what you can see, hear or touch.

Try It: Coming back to the here and now

The chatter in our heads can suck up so much of our attention that it's easy to spend most of our days lost in our thoughts. As often as you can, practise coming back into the here and now by taking a moment to become more aware of what you are perceiving through your senses:

● **Look.** Pause, look around and notice five things you can see. Some parents find it helps to look for a particular category, such as objects of a particular colour, or shadows.

● **Listen.** Listen carefully and identify five sounds you can hear. Perhaps you become aware of distant traffic, birds singing or the almost imperceptible sound of your own breath.

● **Feel.** Notice five things you can feel in contact with your body – your feet on the floor, your legs on the chair, your hair against your face, the texture of your clothes and so on.

Many parents are astonished when they try these exercises and realize how rarely they are fully present in the here and now. One mum told me how tuning in to the sounds outside her living room had made her aware of how much of the time she was completely absorbed in her to-do list. Another decided to unplug her earphones one morning and focus instead on taking in her surroundings as she walked to work. She had never properly looked up before and was amazed by some of the architecture she saw, and the beauty of the clouds.

We can extend this practice to any activity simply by focusing our attention as fully as possible on whatever our senses are perceiving in that moment. We keep some of our awareness resting gently on our breath, and notice any sensations arising in our bodies or thoughts passing through our minds without

Continued . . .

getting too caught up in them. If frustration, boredom or an impulse to do something more 'productive' arises, we simply notice what we're feeling and continue to pay attention to the colours, smells, textures, tastes and sounds. Here are some ideas for simple ways to practise:

● **Tea- or coffee-drinking.** Before you take a sip, feel the warmth of the cup in your hand. Bring your face closer to the cup, take a deep breath and notice the aroma. Take your first sip slowly and savour the flavour. Notice whether it tastes sweet, bitter, smooth or hot before you slowly swallow. Try not to hurry: really savour each sip. When you have finished, notice the warmth you feel inside and any other sensations that arise.

● **Mindful walking.** Pay attention to your surroundings and the sounds you can hear. Notice how walking *feels* – what's it like as your weight passes from one foot to the other? Remember to focus some attention on your breathing and how you feel in your body. Notice each time your mind wanders, and bring your attention gently back to your experience of walking.

● **Waiting in line.** Observe the people around you and take in your surroundings. What can you see and hear? Notice any impatience you may be feeling. Can you just let yourself experience your frustration without trying to change it or push it away? It helps to keep some of your attention focused on your breath. You can do the same while waiting at a red light or in a traffic jam. Can you notice how tightly you are gripping the steering wheel – then take five deep breaths?

● **Ironing.** Notice the grip of the iron in your hand, the movement of your arm and shoulders as you begin to iron, the hiss and heat of the steam, and the pressure you place on the clothes. Notice the scent and colours, the fabric and textures – and how creases vanish and re-form in new patterns with each pass.

- **Taking a shower.** Feel the temperature of the water and the sensation of it running down your skin. Hear the sound it makes as it sprays through the shower rose then gurgles down the plughole. Notice the smell of the shampoo or gel and the sight of the steam rising and droplets forming on the curtain. When thoughts crowd in, bring your awareness back to your senses.

None of these practices requires any extra time – they are all about bringing more attention to what we're already doing, whether it's washing up, reading your child a bedtime story, brushing your teeth or chopping onions.

These may seem like trivial steps, but every time we manage to tune in to our senses more fully in this way is significant. By bringing our awareness into what we're seeing, hearing or feeling more fully, we turn down the volume of the 'frenemy' in our heads and weaken the hold it has over us. If we can remember to do this a few times during the course of a normal day, we'll find it much easier to stay calm and centred on those occasions when we experience anger, anxiety or other difficult feelings bubbling up inside. As often as we can, we remember to take five deep breaths.

Towards a deeper connection

As we begin to develop more awareness of our habitual thoughts, and find little gaps in our stream of thinking, something remarkable starts to happen. We naturally start to question whether the stories we've always believed about ourselves are actually true. We may start to feel a greater sense of trust – in ourselves, and in life. We may find we are less in thrall to habits that no longer serve us. And we start to speak, think and act from a deeper, more confident place. You might not be mindful most of the time, or even very often at all. But each time you remember to pause and take a breath, you're nurturing the seed of calm which we all carry within us, but with which we can easily lose touch in the busyness of day-to-day parenting.

We may notice that each time we connect with this deeper part of ourselves, we feel a greater sense of connection to others – no matter how different they appear on the surface, whether in terms of their appearance or the way they live their lives. Most importantly, we also sense a deeper connection with our children. We might still get angry if they've just spilled their juice all over our new carpet or slammed their bedroom door, but we never lose touch with the unconditional bond we share.

When we start to feel this connection more regularly, we may experience a sense of altruism that goes far beyond our initial goal of feeling a little better in ourselves. We may be more inclined to share a smile, a kind gesture or even a more ambitious contribution to our family, our community or the wider world. And we tend to have greater confidence in our ability to choose an effective response to our everyday parenting dilemmas – whether it's a son in the midst of a meltdown or a daughter who's refusing to speak.

*

The five key points

The 'frenemy' within

- Our busy minds can make parenting harder than it needs to be.

- Mindfulness helps us to stop 'filling in gaps'.

- A mindful pause gives us a chance to respond rather than react.

- Focus on what you can see, hear or feel to come back to the here and now.

- The mind is a master story-teller: don't believe everything it says.

Session 3

The K-word

There are now enough studies demonstrating the positive impact of kindness on our physical and emotional well-being to collapse a bookshelf. The effects are so powerful that some psychologists believe that kindness should rank alongside a balanced diet, regular exercise and quitting smoking as among the basic steps we might take to improve our health. According to Richard Davidson, an American neuroscientist who has spent many years studying compassion, feelings of kindness and generosity sustain positive emotion in the brain more than anything else yet measured in his field. Our heart rate slows, we secrete the 'bonding hormone' oxytocin, and more blood is pumped through the parts of the brain linked to empathy, care-giving and feelings of pleasure. The benefits include:

- greater ability to handle stress

- healthier functioning of the heart

- lasting increase in happiness levels

- less mind-wandering and immersion in negative thoughts

- better relationships

Despite all the wonderful benefits, I often find that with parents I must approach the K-word with extreme caution – and only with careful preparation. However innocent the idea of being a bit nicer to ourselves may sound, it can be very hard to give ourselves permission to put this into practice. The mere mention of self-kindness can trigger these kinds of reactions:

- 'Sounds very unnatural to me.'

- 'Don't be ridiculous – I can't change my personality.'

- 'It sounds selfish.'

- 'I don't have time!'

- 'That's all very well, but I need to put my children first.'

Every mum and dad I see is doing the best they can and wants nothing but the best for their children. Nevertheless, we often speak to ourselves in far harsher tones than we would ever use to a friend who is struggling, and our schedules may rarely feature time to do something just for ourselves. We all seem to suffer from this drought of self-compassion to a certain extent, and I frequently discover that this is one of the most rewarding issues to explore when working with parents. It can be surprisingly difficult to persuade mums and dads to show themselves more kindness, but it can yield huge dividends for them and their families.

In this session, we look at why cultivating a more compassionate attitude towards ourselves is such a good idea, why it can seem so difficult, and the sorts of small, manageable steps we can take to bring more of this magical quality into our daily lives. There's nothing selfish about this process: as we learn to take better care of ourselves, we have a natural tendency to find new ways to care for others, especially our children.

> ## Kindness Is Good for Our Health
>
> In purely physical terms, compassion is so good for us in part
> because it stimulates the Vagus nerve – the 'brake' on the nervous
> system we activate by taking deep, full-bellied breaths, which
> we encountered in Session 1 (see page 19). Having a healthy
> 'Vagal tone' is linked to the efficient functioning of the heart, so
> practising kindness can reduce the risk of heart disease. The
> Vagus nerve also affects how we relate to other people: it's
> linked to nerves that tune our ears to speech, coordinate eye
> contact and regulate emotional expressions. So, along with
> taking five deep breaths, practising compassion is a great way to
> keep your Vagus nerve healthy and tune in to the wisdom of
> your brain, heart and gut – a topic we'll discuss in more depth
> in Session 5.

Why is being kind to ourselves so hard?

We talked in the last session about the way the 'frenemy' in our head
generates a constant stream of thinking: often comprised largely of
fears about the future and regrets about the past. Many parents find
that in all this incessant chatter, one voice tends to dominate – the
harsh tones of a vocal 'inner critic' who is ever eager to dwell on the
negatives and tell us exactly where we're going wrong (often when
we're trying to fall asleep, or when we wake up in the small hours before
the alarm).

We may assume that this voice is helping to motivate us, and tell
ourselves that we won't achieve much if we start cutting ourselves too
much slack. In reality, the 'inner critic' is putting us down and draining
us of the energy we need to tackle our day. We'd get far more done if we
spoke to ourselves with words of encouragement rather than criticism,
but we're so used to listening to our 'inner critic' that we may never

question whether it's really telling us the truth. Even people who are enjoying life and thriving as parents can be plagued by a voice warning that it could all fall apart at any moment – a sneaking suspicion that things are 'too good to last'.

Why do we spend so much time beating ourselves up? From day one, we're programmed to believe we're not good enough. Since our earliest childhood, we've been set up to compete – bombarded with messages telling us that we need to achieve more, work harder, be thinner, look more attractive, earn more money and strive for perfection. When we become parents, the pressure to 'get it right' can seem even greater. The fact you've read this far is already proof that you care about being a good parent. But the 'inner critic' is so stubborn that if I even try to suggest to some parents that they are doing a much better job than they realize, they dismiss what I'm saying by waving a hand and telling me I'm just trying to be nice. I can almost see them thinking, 'That's all very well for you to say – but you wouldn't be so sympathetic if you saw just how impatient I can get with my kid sometimes.'

The problem doesn't stop there. As parents I work with begin to see how hard they can be on themselves, they often start beating themselves up over their habit of beating themselves up. Remember that this is a collective problem: every one of us struggles at some level with accepting ourselves, just as we are.

The seductive dangers of comparison

Since the earliest days of our caveman ancestors, human beings have been social creatures with a powerful urge to connect. Parents naturally look to others for ideas and inspiration – and for a sense of belonging to a wider community. As soon as our children are born, we want to know how they are doing in relation to their peers and that they are passing the right milestones at the right times. It can be very helpful to compare notes with other parents as part of a supportive community, but if we spend too much time focusing on what others are doing, it's easy to start questioning whether we're doing a good enough job.

Social media – despite its many benefits – has turned our natural inclination to compare into an epidemic. Now we're only a click away from somebody who seems to be more accomplished, better looking, wealthier or handling their family life in an enviably relaxed and successful style (often in a picture-postcard setting). Even if we realize at some level that the images we see are carefully filtered, and the lives of our friends may be messier than their status updates or Instagram feeds suggest, the niggling feeling of inferiority can burrow into our minds like a worm.

Such feelings are perfect food for the 'inner critic'. Expert at kicking us when we're down, this voice has an uncanny habit of striking when we least expect. The 'inner critic' loves to compare us unfavourably with others and is constantly finding new targets: whether it be an impeccably attired mum at the school gate, a dad who seems to have it all together, or a celebrity model whose body's back in shape six weeks after having a baby. Even if we succeed in temporarily silencing the voice in one area of our lives, it always seems to pop up in another. Our 'inner critic' knows all our weak spots and is even more difficult to ignore when we're feeling sensitive, tired or vulnerable.

It's not selfish to be kind to yourself

After so many years of being hard on ourselves, practising kindness is not easy. Many of us grew up in households run by parents who found it hard to be kind to themselves, and we may have inherited their self-critical stance without even realizing it, unknowingly depriving ourselves of one of our most valuable resources. We might have learned the lesson early on that putting our own needs first is necessarily selfish in some way – and we may feel this even more strongly when we have children of our own.

We've all heard about the importance of 'putting on your own oxygen mask first' so that you're better able to help others. But there is still often an unspoken assumption in our society that parents should sacrifice everything for their children. Being kind to yourself does not mean being neglectful of your children, selfish, self-indulgent or self-absorbed. It's the precise opposite of wallowing in self-pity. The aim is to take the constructive step of thinking for a moment about how you might be able to comfort and care for yourself at any given time. Nevertheless, mums and dads who do make an occasional attempt to put their own needs first often feel torn: 'It's all very well trying to look after myself, but where's the time?'

I learned the value of self-kindness myself a few years ago when I was going through a particularly tough time. Looking back, I can see I was grieving over the deaths of several loved ones and the break-up of a long-term relationship. But instead of facing my feelings, I spent two years numbing myself with stodgy takeaways, alcohol, partying and flings. As I slowly began to realize, all this running away wasn't the answer and certainly wouldn't make me happy in the long run.

Being kinder to ourselves takes courage. We start to deepen our appreciation of the simple but often forgotten truth that being imperfect, making mistakes and experiencing difficulties are an inevitable part of being a parent. Our vulnerability is nothing to be ashamed of. In fact, facing the tender spots within ourselves helps us to connect with others more deeply, including our children.

Needed: a subtle but profound shift

The irony is that parents tend to be experts at showing kindness to others, but helping them direct some of this kindness inwards is one of the most difficult parts of my job. Some feel angry if I even imply that they might consider showing themselves more compassion, because if it were that simple, they would have done it already. At times, even mentioning the K-word can temporarily make things worse – prompting yet another outburst from the 'inner critic' who is always on stand-by to point out that previous attempts at self-compassion have ended in dismal failure. Everyone knows that work–life balance is important, but self-care can turn into just another out-of-reach target and another reason to feel like we're failing. How many of us think we're getting it right?

Though I often have to put this very diplomatically – sometimes after many sessions of offering reassurance – the reality in many families is that a lack of self-compassion is not only a question of time. Finding space to show ourselves more kindness is about a subtle but profound shift in perspective. We have to make a conscious decision to be nicer to ourselves. We can then see kindness as a skill to practise, albeit one that we may not have learned much about in childhood, and certainly weren't taught in school.

Learning to be kinder to yourself is not something that happens in a flash. Like any habit, it can be cultivated through small, regular steps. It's all about learning to recognize when the 'inner critic' has seized the controls. It would be futile to try to silence this voice permanently and probably not a very good idea: just like other parts of ourselves, it has its unique part to play. But there's no point giving the 'inner critic' more air time than it deserves. Even noticing when it has begun running its old routines immediately starts to weaken its hold.

Your secret superpower: setting intentions

While the mind can often behave like a troublesome 'frenemy', it can also be an incredibly powerful force for generating feelings of well-being – when we remember to take charge. But as we all know, changing long-standing patterns of behaviour can take time. Just as our New Year's resolutions to get to the gym more often or eat healthier food can fall by the wayside, so our commitment to be kinder to ourselves can be hard to maintain. It's worth persevering: bringing more kindness into your life can change your whole experience of parenting for the better.

I have found that one of the most powerful techniques for enlisting the help of the mind – rather than constantly fighting it – is to set an intention: a clear statement of a particular way you want to be in the world. You can then return to this intention whenever you notice your commitment to yourself has started to slip. I find the technique works best if you use an 'I am' statement, for example:

- I am being kinder to myself.

- I am cultivating compassionate thoughts.

- I am finding time to focus on feelings of kindness and compassion.

The key with intention-setting is to really experience the feeling associated with the 'I am' statement as you make it. For example, if your intention is to be kinder to yourself, take a moment to think of a person or animal you care about. Breathe the feeling of kindness into your heart area. Really try to experience the feeling you want to bring into your life as you repeat the intention. This may feel a little strange at first, but deliberately generating feelings in this way will serve to anchor your new way of being in your body, as well as your mind.

You can practise this as many times as you wish. Parents I work with often find it helpful to write their intentions down. You can use the journal at the end of this book (page 259), or write them on postcards and stick them up in a place where you can see them regularly, such as on the fridge or on a wardrobe door. You can begin this practice at any time – though it's also wonderful to take some time to set clear intentions at the start of a new year or on your birthday.

Try not to get too attached to exactly *how* your intention will come about. The important thing is to keep cultivating the feeling associated with your new commitment to yourself. When you review your intentions a year later, you may be surprised at how much has changed.

Try It: Intention-setting ceremony

Creating your own ceremony to set your intentions can be a powerful way to express your new commitments to yourself and embed them in your mind. You can do this alone by setting aside twenty minutes or so in a place where you won't be disturbed, or you can invite friends or family to join in – children love to be included. You can do this at any time of year, or on a special date such as your birthday or New Year's Eve.

● Create your own 'sacred space' on a table or on the floor by arranging some candles, flowers or special objects such as a pendant, photograph, stone or crystal. You can enhance the atmosphere further by dimming the lights, using essential oils or quietly playing relaxing background music. You can also do this outside if you have a garden.

● Take five deep breaths to calm your mind. Drop your attention into your body for a few moments to help centre yourself.

● Reflect on the last year. Think about its highlights and the things that made you most grateful. You may wish to make notes in the journal on page 259. Try to think of at least three good things and spend a few moments thinking or writing in detail about how they happened and why you were so pleased about them.

● Write down on a sheet of paper any habits, beliefs or memories from the past year that you want to release. Tear the paper up into tiny pieces and place them in a special bowl (you can discard them at the end of the ceremony). If you are outside, you may wish safely to burn the piece of paper instead.

- Focus on what intentions you want to set for the next year. There is no rush with this process: let your imagination roam free. Decide what you would like your life to look like in different areas: family, career, health, finances and your relationship with your children. It's good to write your intentions down.

- If you are performing the ceremony with others, you can take turns to state your intentions out loud. You may also wish to say a few words silently or offer a prayer for help in realizing your intentions in your daily life.

- Close the ceremony in whatever way you feel appropriate. If others are present, ask everyone to take a little time once again to say a few words about the things that gave them the most gratitude. End the ceremony by blowing out the candles or turning up the lights and changing the music.

Starting small: planting new thoughts

As with the cultivation of any new habit, the key with kindness is to start small. You don't have to take radical action: begin by reflecting a little on the sorts of thoughts you want to encourage. Like flowers being watered, the more attention you give to them, the more they will thrive.

When I was working through my own difficult times, I found it very helpful to write kind phrases to myself over and over again in my journal. I would repeat them every evening and then I would read them back to myself on the bus to work. I'd also look out for inspiring quotes online or in magazines, and I'd make a note of anything or anyone who inspired me or helped me feel better. Our feelings of unworthiness can be like onions – just when you feel you're getting somewhere, you find another layer. I found that repeating these kind phrases was a powerful way to begin gradually and gently peeling more of those layers away.

Some parents find it helpful to memorize a set of kind phrases they can repeat silently when they feel upset. Though they may jar at first, saying, writing or reading such statements on a regular basis will generate powerful feelings of self-compassion in the long run. Here are some possibilities:

- This is really difficult for me right now.

- Everyone feels this way sometimes.

- May I be kind to myself in this moment.

- I am worthy of giving myself some care.

- It's all okay really.

- You are doing all right.

- Nobody is perfect.

- Just breathe.

- I value myself.

- I am enough.

- Life feels relentless right now and I deserve a break.

- I deserve to be taken care of just as much as the rest of my family.

- I allow myself time to step back and look after myself.

- I work through my difficult feelings at my own pace.

- We are all in this together.

Cues to be kind

As you begin to weave such phrases into your daily life, it can be helpful to give yourself a little nudge to remember them at regular intervals. Here are some possible cues:

- Carry an **object** that reminds you to be kind to yourself, such as a special stone or pendant. Or perhaps a memento from someone you love.

- Stick **Post-it notes** with inspiring quotes or kind phrases around the house. You could put them on the fridge, by the bed, by the kettle, or make notes on your phone or in your journal. Or use a **white board** with coloured pens.

- Select a **cue moment** to rehearse one of the quotes. It could be just before you sit down to eat, before you read your child a story or every time you close the front door.

*

From words to actions

Repeating kind phrases is a powerful practice – but seemingly small *acts* of kindness to oneself can make an even bigger difference. Raising the next generation is the most important job anyone can do: value yourself enough to make sure you sometimes do things that you enjoy. The very act of making a conscious decision to show yourself some compassion in the way you might to a child, friend or animal can make a big difference to how you feel. Here are some suggestions:

- Phone or text a friend you have been meaning to contact for ages and organize a catch-up.

- Buy yourself a treat, such as flowers, chocolates or a magazine.

- Go for a walk, get some fresh air or do some gardening.

- Take a long bubble bath, inhaling the fragrances.

- Walk barefoot on grass or soil.

- Take five deep breaths.

- Linger over a cup of tea or your favourite coffee.

- Come up with some inspiring songs on Spotify or iTunes that reflect kindness. Share playlists with your friends or family.

- Watch something that used to make you laugh – live comedy is great, but clips on YouTube are also a wonderful way to reconnect with that lighter part of yourself.

- Put your hands over your heart or give yourself a hug – something you can do in private if you feel self-conscious. These gestures can be surprisingly powerful and can help us get out of our busy chattering minds and into our bodies. (See Session 4.)

- Some parents make a 'Kindness Wall' where family members make a note of kind acts they have performed or received during the week – a great way to share the benefits.

- Finally, meditation can be really helpful and there is strong evidence for its benefits. There are many forms – from the simple mindfulness exercises described in this book to more formal periods of sitting quietly, practising yoga or walking mindfully in nature. (See Resources, pages 241–2 and 251–5.)

Such steps will not only help you to foster greater compassion for yourself – you will also be modelling self-care for your children.

> ## Rosemary: 'It was about giving myself permission'
>
> *'I like swimming, I know it's good for me and I know all its benefits – but I'd stopped going. My friend told me that I don't value myself enough to make it a priority. I'm juggling so much – making sure my kids get to their after-school clubs, tidying up after others, organizing shopping or meals – and it slips off the agenda. But going back felt amazing. It was about giving myself permission to spend this time on me. Now it's part of my routine and I know it's good for me.'*

*

Sending kindness into the world

The wonderful thing about compassion is that it works in all directions – like a miniature sun that lights everything touched by its rays. Self-compassion cannot help but inspire feelings of expansiveness and generosity: as you start to go easier on yourself, you'll naturally find yourself feeling kinder towards others. It can be a powerful practice to make a more conscious effort to foster this kind of altruism beyond your immediate circle, even if you only take baby steps. We've all experienced how even the briefest of smiles or a moment of authentic connection with a stranger can brighten your and someone else's day, but it's easy to miss such chances when our schedules feel so crammed. Nevertheless, it's good to remember that at the deepest level we are all connected – and every act of kindness makes a difference.

Matthieu Ricard is a Buddhist monk who has been dubbed the 'world's happiest man' after brain-imaging studies suggested he possessed almost supernatural reserves of tranquillity. He has recommended spending ten seconds silently wishing happiness on strangers you pass in the street or sit next to on the bus. The positive effects on your own mind linger for some time after you have chosen these kind thoughts. Ricard compares the afterglow to the scent that lingers after you briefly open a bottle of perfume.

Cultivating compassion is not about seeking approval or some kind of reward from others. Family or friends might not comment on or even seem to notice your new perspective – and that doesn't matter. The important thing is to pay attention to how *you* feel as you consciously practise being kinder to yourself and others.

Try It: Sending out loving kindness

We set the intention to be kind, compassionate and loving to all beings – including ourselves – even if we aren't feeling particularly generous towards anybody in that moment.

● Begin by sitting or lying in a comfortable, relaxed position. You may wish to close your eyes and place your hand over your heart. Bring your awareness to your breath, and notice any sensations in your body. You may wish to set a timer for a minute or two. Silently repeat the following phrases:

'May I be happy.'
'May I feel safe and protected.'
'May I be strong.'
'May I be peaceful.'
'May I live with kindness.'

● If any of the above phrases does not speak to you, then you can replace it with words that resonate more strongly – perhaps related to a desire for more inspiration, insight or calm.

● As you repeat these phrases, notice any feelings that arise. Some parents are kind to themselves so rarely that this exercise can feel awkward at first. The 'frenemy' mind may resist these statements, complaining that you are certainly *not* feeling any of these positive qualities. Persist with the practice. Just as a friend might wish you well, you can too.

● Notice what comes up as you continue the affirmations. Some people encounter feelings of frustration, irritability or anger. It's also possible that you will start to feel an inner softening, or even sadness, as you direct compassion inwards. Notice whatever feeling arises, allow it to be, and continue with the silent phrases.

● When you feel ready, adapt the same phrases to send kindness and understanding to somebody else – perhaps your child, a partner or a friend. Again, notice how you are feeling as you send loving, benevolent thoughts their way.

● In the final stage of the exercise, you can broaden your compassion practice to include a larger community – your family, a school, your workplace or even the country or planet as a whole.

● If you are facing challenges with a particular individual, it can be a very powerful practice to focus loving kindness on them. This doesn't mean you approve or condone their actions; it's merely a way of showing that your compassion for a fellow human transcends whatever differences you may be having. You do this to keep your own heart open – not to change anybody else.

The wonderful thing about kindness is that it has such a strong ripple effect. This principle was beautifully illustrated by a teacher at a south-east London primary school who organized pupils to attach handwritten, uplifting notes to copies of the *Metro* newspaper. Some of the readers were so moved that they wrote letters of appreciation, which in turn multiplied the feelings of goodwill. This was only one aspect of a much wider Kindness Project in Schools, initiated by Action for Happiness, an organization aiming to promote a kinder society, in collaboration with Bernadette Russell, author of *Do Nice, Be Kind, Spread Happy*, a book about acts of kindness for children. Here are some other recent examples of kind acts by strangers in Britain that had such a big impact on individuals that they made the news:

- In January 2015, a man on a train to Bristol handed a young mother with a three-year-old £5 for a drink and a handwritten note calling her a 'credit to your generation' and praising her parenting skills. The twenty-three-year-old mother said her anonymous benefactor's generosity had made her want to cry.

- In December 2015, a seven-year-old boy from Aberdeen asked his friends and family to donate food to a local food bank rather than give him any birthday presents since he felt sad about people who could not afford meals and he had enough toys. His mum said he was 'chuffed' with the 70kg pile of goods he was able to donate.

- In May 2016, a mother took to Facebook to thank a member of staff at a supermarket in Basingstoke who had helped her with her young daughters who were having a meltdown at the check-out. The woman lightened the mood by allowing one of the girls – both of whom are registered as blind and have autism – to help scan the items. 'This very kind lady decided to help instead of judge,' the mother posted. 'It melts my heart to come across people that are prepared to go the extra mile – and little acts of kindness make a massive difference to my world.' Her post gained half a million 'likes'.

While these kinds of striking stories illustrate the enormous power of kindness, it is arguably the little-noticed, consistent, everyday actions that have an even more profound impact. It can be the simplest of gestures – such as stopping to chat to a lonely-looking mum in the playground – that can make all the difference.

> ## Hannah: 'I did the best I could to reassure her'
>
> *'I started chatting in the playground to Kate, another mum, who looked really stressed and upset. Kate opened up to me and told me it had been the fifth morning in a row that her eight-year-old had shouted and screamed at her and she couldn't get him to sit down and eat breakfast or get dressed. Kate is tired, blames herself and takes her son's words and behaviour personally. I did the best I could to reassure her and I think it gave her a little lift. Taking a moment to do this made me feel good too.'*

Gratitude: compassion's transformative twin

We probably all have a childhood memory of being told to 'count our blessings'. The phrase arguably ranks alongside 'worse things happen at sea' or 'there's no point crying over spilt milk' in the top ten irritating clichés that only make us feel worse. Come to think of it, 'When life hands you lemons, make lemonade' is also a strong contender.

However, it would be a mistake to dismiss the profound power of gratitude. Just as neuroscientists have confirmed what sages always knew when it comes to kindness, the results of studies into gratitude have been equally striking. Pioneering research in this relatively new field has shown the many benefits that taking a moment to be thankful can have for our bodies and minds, including:

- more optimism, happiness and joy

- stronger immune systems and lower blood pressure

- fewer feelings of loneliness and isolation

- acting with greater generosity and compassion

- fewer symptoms of depression

The good news is that you don't even need to identify anything in particular to be grateful for. The very act of trying to think about something good in your life encourages your brain to secrete the feel-good neurotransmitter serotonin (the active ingredient in a number of commonly prescribed antidepressants). With a little practice, you can quickly establish a virtuous cycle in which the brain starts automatically to scan for more and more reasons to be grateful. Some of the parents I work with are surprised at how much better they feel when they actively start to appreciate the little things in life – such as meeting up with a friend for a coffee or sharing a joke with their child. Taking a moment to appreciate what you already have – rather than focusing on what you feel is missing – can provide a real lift, especially on bad days when you're stressed and tired.

As with compassion, gratitude is a wonderful habit to nurture. Here are some tips to bring more of this quality into your daily life:

- **Gratitude diary.** Make it a habit to jot down in your journal a few things that have gone well that day. You need only do this two or three times a week. As you write, dwell on the positive feelings you experience. The more detail you can include as to why you are grateful for each entry, the better.

- **Rituals.** Perform little rituals to remind you to focus on the positives. For example, before eating dinner, each member of the family could take a turn to identify something they are happy about. Or you could create a 'gratitude jar', with each family member putting in a marble each day to represent something good that's happened. Children love these kinds of games as they give them a glimpse into their parents' world.

- **Gratitude 'first aid kit'.** If something triggers old, negative feelings, or puts your 'frenemy' mind into overdrive, it can be helpful to shift your mood by thinking about the many things that have gone well in the past.

● **Thank-you notes.** The habit of writing thank-you notes may have gone out of fashion in the digital age, but writing short notes to somebody who has been helpful, or in return for a gift, is a powerful way to express gratitude.

● **Delivering a 'gratitude letter'.** Write a detailed letter to a relative, friend or mentor – someone who has inspired, helped or supported you. Deliver the letter in person and you may feel the most intense wave of gratitude you have ever experienced. The recipient is almost certain to be profoundly moved by such a special gesture.

● **Gratitude apps.** There are a number of excellent gratitude apps designed to help parents identify the good things that have happened each day. (See Resources, page 256).

Giving yourself permission

Starting consciously to bring more kindness and gratitude into your daily life through thoughts and actions is an excellent practice. If this works for you, you might consider taking a further step by exploring ways to carve out a little more time for yourself in the course of a busy week.

This can be particularly helpful if you are feeling that it's a struggle to adjust to the inevitably big changes that becoming a parent involves. These can affect people in many different ways. Some mourn the loss of their independence, while others eagerly embrace a whole new perspective on life – with many parents somewhere in between, struggling to find a balance.

The question isn't really whether you have lost or gained, but how you feel about yourself right now and whether you believe you are embodying the values you want to stand for in your life today. Amid all the pressures of parenting, it can make a huge difference if you can give yourself permission to set aside even a small amount of time to do something that 'lights you up' in some way – perhaps an activity you used to enjoy but have given up since you started work, got married or had children.

Here are some techniques I use with mums and dads to help them reconnect with the parts of themselves beyond their role as parents:

● Find a simple outlet for expressing creativity without feeling any need to perform or impress. For example, you could draw, enjoy a mindful colouring book, make music, sing, dance, write, take photographs, sew, knit, make pottery, arrange flowers or paint. Allowing yourself to become absorbed in any form of creative activity is one of the most powerful ways to focus your mind on something different, and can leave you feeling inspired and refreshed.

● Create a weekly ritual that allows you to spend some time alone. Sticking as far as possible to the same day and time will help make this into a habit.

● Ask yourself: 'What change can I embrace right now to make me happier?' Whether the change is at home, at work, finding a new hobby or volunteering, your next step is to take action.

● Identify goals beyond your role as parent. These could range from plans to study or start a business to completing a 5k run or joining a book club.

● There may be ways to find time to enjoy doing something that you did before the children arrived – even if you can only manage to do it for a short time. Possibilities might include:

    ● Playing a sport/hiking/rock-climbing or adventure sports
    ● Joining a choir or kirtan chanting group
    ● Exercise classes – yoga, Pilates, Zumba or gym

- Gardening or taking walks in nature
- A spa day with friends
- Cinema or theatre trips
- Connecting with spiritual communities
- Cake-baking groups or other shared activities for parents
- Joining supportive online parenting communities

Arranging such activities might sound like a big ask – after all, if it were easy to take these kinds of breaks, every parent would be doing it. It doesn't matter if your plans sometimes get cancelled at the last minute or have to be changed: the important thing is gradually to shift your mindset by recognizing that making a little time for yourself is a vital part of parenting, and your whole family will benefit.

*

Lisa: 'I just want a bit of "me" back'

'I know I'm exhausted. I know I have a tendency to look on the gloomy side of life. I think maybe that partly came from my mum – she was always critical of my boyfriends and she placed a really high value on looks. My dad was quite strict, almost like one of those Victorian dads. He never expressed his feelings, and I never really had much confidence. I know I blame myself for my fifteen-year-old Emily's problems, but I can't see how I can stop that. I can't help it. It's just the way I am.'

When I asked Lisa where the fun was in her life, she looked at me and cried, *'I don't have fun any more. I just want a bit of "me" back.'*

I worked with Lisa to find some phrases that spoke to her, even though at first they felt a little awkward. She came up with the following affirmations and saved them on her phone:

Continued . . .

- *You're only human. I know you're feeling really stressed right now, but this will pass.*

- *This feeling is only temporary.*

- *Things can get better, and they have got better. Just take it day by day.*

- *You've got some really nice things to look forward to.*

As we explored her feelings more deeply, Lisa began to see that it would be okay for her to take a break. It wasn't just her busy schedule that was holding her back, but her false belief that showing herself some kindness would undermine her performance as a mum.

We worked out a few things that wouldn't take too much time that she would enjoy – including an evening reconnecting with girlfriends. Lisa had done an art degree and once enjoyed painting. One Sunday, she gave herself an hour to get her easel out of the loft and have a go at painting again. Her face came alive as she described the feeling of rediscovering the neglected, creative part of herself.

'It felt so good to be doing something artistic again. Hours passed and it just took my mind off all the stressful things that had been happening. I've noticed that when I'm more relaxed, Emily's also a little better and is taking a bit more responsibility. This kindness practice is a new thing for me and I'm helping Emily learn to do it for herself as well. It feels good to laugh again.'

The five key points
The K-word

- Science shows that kindness is good for your body and brain.

- It's not selfish to give yourself a break: your kids will benefit.

- Setting intentions is your secret superpower.

- Make kindness a habit: every small action makes a difference.

- Gratitude for simple things is an instant mood-lifter.

Session
4

Out of our heads, into our bodies

Not so long ago, I was walking up the high street when a young woman working for a luxury beauty brand flashed me a smile and complimented me on my appearance. Within a few moments, she had deftly steered me to a counter where another young sales assistant was lurking. 'Have you thought about an eye cream?' she asked. 'What do you use at the moment?' Her demeanour hardened as she pursed her lips, scrutinized me more closely and asked how old I was. 'You don't have *too* many lines,' she said, though her pained expression suggested otherwise. She produced a mirror; in the high magnification my eyes did indeed seem to be far more creased than I'd imagined. I found myself looking at the creams on offer – which were well out of my price range. I had been having a pretty good day until I had stepped into the shop. Suddenly, I was feeling insecure. To cheer myself up, I bought a chocolate bar.

Never being good enough – so many of us struggle with this feeling, and it often plays out in relation to our appearance. Everywhere we look – from adverts for beauty products and miracle diets to the latest exercise fad or cosmetic surgery – we're bombarded with the message that we need to make ourselves more attractive. We can't walk past a supermarket checkout without being confronted with images of celebrity perfection on the magazine rack, or we check our phones while waiting to pay and absorb a stream of carefully filtered pictures on Facebook of other mums and dads looking their immaculate best.

In short, we live in a society that's always giving us a new reason to worry about whether we are fit, thin or good-looking enough. This can become even more pronounced for women who've had children, when we may notice cellulite, stretch marks, varicose veins and put on weight. It's no wonder so many of us feel insecure – and when you're feeling tired and vulnerable it can be harder to remain positive, or resist the temptation to click on pictures of have-it-all mums or wonder how other dads manage to make so much time for the gym. Few things are liable to drive our 'inner critic' into a frenzy faster than worries about how we look.

It's become a cliché to say that the path to inner peace lies within. Yet there is a deep truth hidden in this simple statement. There is great power in learning to see beyond appearances – our own and other people's – and connect to the basic goodness we all share at our core. In this session, we explore how we can begin to relate differently to our difficult feelings by getting out of our heads and tuning in to our bodies. We discover how to use the body as an anchor to bring us back to the here and now. And we look at some more ways in which the breath – our ever-present ally – can be used to help deal with specific challenges.

A new relationship with our feelings

In today's world, we tend to spend most of our time in our heads. We're so preoccupied by the thoughts running through our minds that it's almost as if we live life from the 'neck up'. We're like heads on sticks: our bodies are merely vehicles for transporting our brain between meetings. This seems normal because everyone's doing it – but it's what's making us all so stressed.

Just as it's easy to overlook the power of the breath, it's easy to lose touch with what it feels like fully to inhabit our bodies. This happens to almost all of us to some extent, but is particularly common when we've suffered some form of physical or emotional trauma. Even for those of us who've made it through life relatively unscathed, as parents we may be so busy looking after our children that we barely have time to look after ourselves. Our bodies are constantly giving us vital messages about how we are feeling and what we need, but many of us are just too busy or overwhelmed to pay much attention. We may only start to listen when something goes wrong, when we suffer an injury or fall ill.

This disconnect comes at a price: we lose touch with our feelings. Though we tend to focus most of our attention on what's going on in our heads, our emotions happen in our bodies. Anger, sadness, frustration and fear all occur as physical sensations – often arising in our head, chest, stomach or throat. This very physical basis of our emotions is reflected in the language we use when we talk about how we feel: the 'punch in the gut' of disappointment when our child misses out on a place on a sports team, or the 'butterflies' fluttering in our stomach as we watch the curtain rising on their first school play. We may not always have a name for these sensations, or know why they are happening, but they do much to determine the quality of our life.

Our thoughts and feelings are closely linked. Whether it's chest-tightening sadness, a hot flash of anger or the screw of anxiety turning in our gut – these sensations act as triggers, setting off a chain reaction of negative thinking. We can get trapped in a vicious cycle as this negative thinking in turn makes the feelings more intense. Before we know it, we're putting ourselves down, replaying the same old scripts, and we feel even worse. We simply don't know how to break free.

It's only natural that we look for ways to cope – often by distracting or numbing ourselves in some way. We all know the signs: comfort-eating cakes and biscuits, one too many glasses of wine, hours on Facebook and Instagram, blow-outs in the shops, gorging on TV box sets, caffeine binges or even just keeping ourselves constantly on the go. There's obviously nothing wrong with any of these things in moderation – we all do them, and a lot of the time they're great fun. But it's worth asking yourself whether you sometimes use these kinds of activities to take the edge off uncomfortable feelings that you're finding difficult to face.

When I struggled with problems in the past, I know that I had a tendency to get very analytical and try to think myself into feeling better. Of course it's good to think things through, but too much analysing can also become a trap if we take it too far. Working with parents, I began to see that many mums and dads would over-analyse in a similar way. Though they could tell themselves they were working on their problems, in reality they were using all the endless thinking to distract themselves from having to experience their difficult feelings – just as I had once done. We've all been trained since our first day at school to be problem-solvers and rational thinkers, and we need these vital skills to function as parents. But sometimes we get stuck on a merry-go-round – and before long we feel like we're going mad. We're so busy listening to our heads that we've lost touch with how we truly *feel* in our bodies.

If we're really honest with ourselves, we often see that all of these strategies are only ever short-term fixes. Pushing our feelings down, distracting ourselves or endlessly analysing unfortunately do not get rid of our emotional pain – in fact, it often comes back with more zing. We can go about our day pretending to the world and ourselves that we're okay, but it's exhausting always to be wearing a mask.

The key to finding greater balance in our lives is to foster a new relationship with our feelings. Rather than looking for ways to shut down, we gradually learn to meet even our most difficult emotions with an attitude of curiosity, acceptance and kindness. This is not easy at first, but as we practise we may start to discover that our fear, shame or anger are not as overwhelming as we might have once feared. However intense they might at first seem, as we face them they gradually start to lose their power.

If this sounds to you like a tall order, you're right: this is a radical break with how most of us usually operate. It's understandable that some of the parents I work with worry about what might happen if they drop their guard and start to allow themselves to experience their true feelings more fully: 'I'll be a total mess, I'll fall apart – and how will that help my family?' In reality, such worries are rarely justified, and mums and dads often discover a newfound sense of clarity by investigating the feelings they would prefer to avoid, just like the sunshine that follows a storm. The important thing is to trust your instincts and only go at a pace that feels right for you.

Some parents may not feel this work is right for them – and that's fine. Others may feel they could benefit from working with a skilled therapist or supportive group, and that's okay too. However, when we do begin to remember to tune in to our body more deliberately – whether it's while we're washing up, reading a bedtime story or doing the school run – we often discover that any tension or discomfort we encounter is not as bad as we might have feared. We see more clearly that our emotions are always changing, much like the weather, and that all of them will eventually pass. And we learn to accept the messages our feelings may have for us without running away.

Try It: Checking in with yourself

Sit up as straight as you can without forcing yourself, with your feet flat on the ground. Relax your shoulders and imagine a thread connected to the top of your head pulling it up towards the ceiling. Place your hands loosely in your lap. You can close your eyes if you like, or simply lower your gaze to the ground. Become aware of the feel of the chair and your feet on the floor.

● Take a moment to tune in to what's going on in your mind and body right now. Notice what kind of thoughts you are having. How are you feeling? Is there tiredness, sadness, or perhaps irritability or frustration? Are there any physical sensations: tension, tightness or discomfort, warmth or cold, tingling or numbness? The goal is not to try to change anything or push anything away – just to turn your attention to what is going on for you in this moment.

● Bring your attention to your breath. It may help to place your hands gently on your belly, feeling it rise and fall. As you inhale, notice the feeling of the air being drawn into your nostrils. Notice how your ribcage gently moves, how your abdomen expands and how your lungs fill with air. As you exhale through your mouth, notice the feeling of the air – perhaps it's warmer as you breathe out. Feel the ribcage and your abdomen relax. Continue to feel the gentle movement of your belly with your hands.

● As you bring your attention back to the breath, your mind will inevitably start to wander. This is normal, and the fact that you've noticed it shows you are already becoming more aware. Whenever you notice that you are starting to get caught up in thinking, gently refocus on the breath.

● As you breathe, broaden the focus of your attention to the body as a whole. Take your time as you become aware of your posture, your facial expression and any sensations – inside the body or on your skin. As your awareness expands, it's as if you're breathing into every part of your body.

● Notice the various sensations you are experiencing: your contact with the floor, your contact with the chair, the feel of your hands in your lap, the posture you're holding and the scents surrounding you – some familiar, some perhaps not. It's as if you're surveying the whole landscape of your body's feelings.

Continued . . .

● When you are ready, begin to wiggle your fingers and toes, then open your eyes and spend a few moments taking in the room.

The beauty of this 'check-in' is that it takes only a few moments and can be done anywhere. It's easier to begin to experiment with dropping into your body in this way when you're feeling relatively calm. As you do this more often, you will start to experience a sense of groundedness that will help you weather the daily stresses and strains of parenting, especially if you can manage to perform it once or twice a day.

Curiosity: our lost treasure

One of the most wonderful blessings of being a parent is watching the way a young child approaches the world with such natural curiosity. The simplest objects can be a source of endless fascination, while plants, flowers and animals spark awestruck delight. We were all like that once, but at some point in our lives the world starts to lose its sparkle. With adult responsibilities to meet, it's all too easy to stop asking questions and lose touch with the sense of wonder and inquisitiveness alive in the eyes of every child.

Though it may lie dormant, our curiosity never dies. As adults, we can rekindle this quality as a powerful ally to help us cope at difficult moments – if only we make a little effort to reawaken our birthright. Rather than running away from or suppressing our difficult feelings, we can choose to investigate them with an open, enquiring mind, tapping into our innate fearlessness and belief in ourselves. We learn to take a closer look at what's happening inside us – much as a curious child inspects a bug in a jar, or carefully looks at the face of a stranger. The simple act of meeting our feelings with curiosity like this opens the door to a new way of being in the world – we start to feel lighter, more at ease and freer.

Harnessing the power of curiosity is not always easy. Our minds have an in-built tendency to resist our sadness, anger or fear and label them as 'bad', and then talk us into spending our energy on trying to get away from them, rather than getting to know them. But the more we resist a feeling, the more it persists. Like a person knee-deep in quicksand, the harder we struggle, the deeper we sink.

As you begin to experiment with meeting your feelings with greater curiosity, be patient with yourself. It helps to remember that being more open to what you are feeling does not mean you have to like it. If you're going through a rough patch, it certainly doesn't mean passively resigning yourself to feeling miserable without doing anything to change your situation. It simply means that you are willing to allow what is happening for you in *that particular moment* rather than creating more inner tension by struggling against it. By being curious, we make a little more space for a feeling that's already happening in the here and now. We're moving with the current of life, rather than against it.

When we cultivate this attitude of curiosity, we stop running away from ourselves. We begin to recognize that everyone has messy feelings to deal with, and there is no such thing as the perfect parent or the perfect family – and that's what makes us human. We become more familiar with the way in which our feelings – however uncomfortable they seem – are constantly in flux. Sometimes they are intense, sometimes much lighter, but we hold a deeper knowing that the only constant is change.

I know from my own journey through grief and anxiety that the more you can connect with your unwanted feelings – as opposed to numbing them – the more alive you will start to feel. I also know that there is no need to rush this process: it's the work of a lifetime. Little by little, as you learn to embrace your lows, you will gradually find that you discover a greater capacity to revel in the highs. As one of my teachers says, the depth of your sorrow is the height of your joy.

*

When you're feeling overwhelmed

One of the reasons we can find our feelings difficult to manage is that our body, brain and nervous system store the emotional residue of adverse experiences or traumas dating back to our early childhood. That's why it's so easy to over-react to a relatively trivial challenge with intense feelings of fear, despair or anxiety that seem out of all proportion to the situation – and we don't even know why. This helps to explain why parents often tell me that it wasn't a thought that triggered a panic attack or a feeling of being overwhelmed – it started with a feeling in the body.

One of the simplest and most effective ways to calm yourself in such a situation is to remember to breathe deeply, preferably five times to start with (harnessing the relaxation response of our old friend the Vagus nerve). There are also a number of techniques we can use to deal with specific challenges, adapted here from the Comprehensive Resource Model of therapy developed by Lisa Schwarz. (For more details, see page 125).

CRM Ocean Breathing: to calm body and mind

This technique generates a feeling of inner peace by helping to regulate and synchronize heart-rate activity and brain waves.

- Breathe in through the nose to the count of five, then out through the mouth to the count of five, *without pausing* between the exhale and the inhale. Continue for as long as desired.

CRM Earth Breathing: for feeling grounded

This technique is good for calming down if ever you feel overwhelmed.

- Imagine energy from deep in the earth coming up into the sole of one of your feet, spiralling up the receiving leg to the base of the spine. Hold the breath there for four or five seconds, then exhale down the other leg and foot back into the earth. Continue until you feel grounded.

CRM Heart Breathing: sending love to ourselves and others

This exercise is used whenever we wish to nurture loving feelings for ourselves or somebody else, and can quickly generate emotional warmth, connectedness and compassion.

- As you breathe in, imagine you are simultaneously drawing breath down from the sky through the crown of your head, and up from the ground through both feet. Inhale the breath into your heart.

- Hold the breath in all four chambers of the heart for four seconds, then exhale out of the front and back of the heart at the same time.

- As you exhale, you can send this 'heart breath' to yourself, your child, your partner or anyone else. Practise as many times as feels right for you.

- You can 'heart breathe' at any time to generate feelings of kindness for yourself, or strengthen your HEART-centred connection with somebody else.

*

Gemma: 'I learned to sit with my feelings'

'I've got two children – a nine-year-old son and an eleven-year-old daughter. They always seem to be squabbling over something – it's really trying. I wish we didn't always end up in arguments every night over such trivial things. It's exhausting and leaves a terrible atmosphere in the house which can last for hours. The children are just relentless

Continued...

and keep going on and on about how unfair everything is. They even use a kind of blackmail on me, saying things like if I really loved them I would give them more time on their mobile phones and stop nagging them about homework. They don't seem to understand that doing well at school is important for their future. It's a constant battle.

'I'm not a good sleeper, so I often wake up feeling drained and I find myself getting so upset and irritated. My boss doesn't seem to understand I'm a human being with a family and not a robot.

'I just exist at the moment. I don't feel I have any life. I'm so tired I can't think straight. Sometimes I just feel like walking out – which I would never do, but that's how I feel. Why can't my children just get on with each other, respect me, and we could have a normal, happy, family life?'

As Gemma talks, she tells me how guilty she feels for having all these negative feelings about her family life when she and her husband had so desperately wanted their children. They had struggled for years through several miscarriages followed by emotionally draining fertility treatments. She was over the moon when her children were born and cherishes them more than she could ever have imagined, but she wonders whether she and her husband ever had a chance to work through the difficult feelings that surfaced during their years of trying for a family.

'To be honest, I've never been able to open up to my friends about this,' Gemma says. *'I hate feeling like a failure – and I'm ashamed that I can't seem to appreciate and enjoy everything I have when I know it's what I always wanted.'*

I ask Gemma what kind of physical sensations she experiences when she is stressed. At first she doesn't understand what I mean. We spend some moments sitting quietly, and I ask her to tune in to her body. She immediately recognizes a familiar tightness in her chest and explains that she often gets headaches.

I encourage Gemma to explore the tightness in her chest more carefully. It feels uncomfortable at first to stay with the feeling, but she practises CRM Earth Breathing and goes at her own pace. After a few minutes, the feeling is still there but seems less intense – almost as if there is now some 'space' around it.

Gradually, over the following weeks, Gemma practises sitting with her feelings in this way when she can grab a spare five minutes after the kids have gone to bed. Keeping herself grounded through the CRM Earth Breathing really helps her to stay calm. She realizes she's more able to cope with the difficult feelings that arise when her children argue and that there's no need to wade in to resolve every squabble.

'I've learned to intervene less often and let my children sort their bickering out for themselves – they can learn a lot more that way about how to resolve conflict,' Gemma says. *'But the bigger lesson has been that I've learned to tune in to how I'm feeling – and I can keep myself grounded in the here and now. I still feel the fear – but it's not quite so scary.'*

Sinking deeper roots within

Our bodies are where our feelings happen – but, as we've seen, so much of the time we're lost in the thoughts in our heads. Learning to meet our feelings with curiosity and acceptance can go a long way to redressing this imbalance, but there are also more formal techniques for finding our way back to our bodies, from yoga and martial arts to many forms of meditation and, of course, sports like running, swimming or cycling. These can all be fantastic ways to inhabit our bodies more fully, but we don't need to go to the local Pilates studio or gym. All we have to do is pay more attention to the underlying sense of aliveness that runs through every part of ourselves – even if we're too distracted most of the time to notice it's there.

Let's try it now. The easiest way is to start with the hands. Hold your palms close together – without touching. What do they feel like? Can you sense a faint tingle – the life energy flowing through and between them? Is it possible to extend your awareness of this 'aliveness' to other areas? Your arms, legs and feet?

This is a subtle but powerful practice. As we tune in to our body more often, we take back some of the attention that is usually entirely filled by the thought-chatter in our mind. The 'frenemy' in our head will continue to tell its stories, but we won't be quite so prone to buying into them.

If you want to take this further, you can try a more formal 'body scan' meditation as recommended by many mindfulness teachers, a version of which is described in the box below. (For some recommended resources for exploring more formal meditations of this kind, see pages 241–2 and 251–5.)

Try It: Body scan

The 'body scan' is a key component of a formal mindfulness meditation practice. The idea is to sweep your attention through different parts of your body in turn, noticing how each part feels and any sensations that arise. As always in mindfulness, we greet anything we encounter with openness and curiosity, gradually going more deeply into our feelings rather than trying to shut them down or change anything.

● Lie comfortably on a soft mat or on your bed (I like to cover myself with a cosy blanket and close my eyes). Begin by focusing your attention at the top of your head and then move down the entire body, focusing on your neck, shoulders, arms, hands, torso, legs, knees and feet.

● Notice any sensations such as tension, warmth, coolness, tingling, pulsing, numbness, throbbing and so on. Your mind will start wandering: making comments, passing judgements or generating thoughts about the past or future. Each time you notice your mind straying, gently bring your attention back to the body part you remember focusing on last.

● After scanning up and down the length of your body a few times, you can move to a more generalized, spacious awareness of your body as a whole. By becoming more familiar with what it feels like to inhabit your body more fully in this way, you will be better able to keep some of your attention rooted within as you go about your day.

I advise parents who wish to explore this in more depth to use a guided audio recording – easily available via a wide variety of CDs, websites or apps – to lead them through the exercise step by step. A full body scan can take forty-five minutes to an hour, but it's equally valuable to try to drop into your body as many times as you remember each day. This helps to anchor us in the present moment and ensures we don't get completely taken over by the stories of the ever-present 'frenemy' in our heads.

*

The five key points

Out of our heads, into our bodies

- All parents face challenging emotions at some point – this is normal.

- Mindfulness helps us to relate to our difficult feelings in new ways.

- Change happens when we get out of our heads and into our bodies.

- When we learn to face our feelings, they lose their power.

- We can use our breath to help if we ever feel overwhelmed.

Getting to know your 'inner parent'

Every parent has heard the saying that it takes a village to raise a child. In tribal societies, boys and girls were expected to start contributing to their community as soon as they could walk – fetching water, foraging for nuts and berries or looking after their even tinier siblings. The whole concept of 'childhood' as we know it today is a relative newcomer on the human stage, and the conventional wisdom about how best to bring up children seems to change with each passing decade.

We can all picture a stern Victorian parent insisting that children should be seen and not heard. Even as late as 1928, the influential American psychologist John B. Watson wrote a popular book called *Psychological Care of Infant and Child* in which he advised parents to withhold affection so as not to 'spoil' their children. He believed that the ideal version of the parent–child relationship should be cool and businesslike – perhaps best symbolized by his recommendation to parents to dress their children like adults and shake hands with them each morning.

By the end of the Second World War, attitudes had started to shift.

The renowned paediatrician Dr Benjamin Spock encouraged mothers to leave stern Victorian attitudes behind and be as generous as possible with their warmth and love. Though controversial in many respects, Spock's *Baby and Child Care*, published in 1946, became one of the bestselling books of all time and its emphasis on parental instincts and intuition shapes attitudes to this day. In the 1950s, John Bowlby's seminal research on 'attachment' demonstrated the importance of the mother–child bond for a child's healthy emotional development and cemented the move away from the strict, punitive parenting school of the previous century.

Since then, an array of new styles has developed, each championed by different experts – from the relaxed and flexible 'permissive parenting' of the 1960s to the rise of the more strategy-based techniques of the 'naughty step' and 'reward charts' popularized in more recent years. We can all now agree that kids need limits and boundaries to feel safe – but, equally, there's a growing recognition that not all strategies will work for all children at all times. Nobody denies the importance of an emotional connection with our children and the need to give them space to express their unique identity. At the same time, the wealth of choices to make and the deluge of information on offer poses parents with new dilemmas. Nobody wants to turn the clock back, but how do we know we're on the right track?

I recently met a mum who voiced concerns I've heard many times in my work with parents. She was so committed to getting her relationship with her son exactly 'right' that she found herself constantly assailed by worries about what might – or might not – be going on in his head. She experienced a stream of thoughts such as: 'I feel there's something he's not telling me. Does he even like me? I've not got the emotional connection "right".' It was almost as if parenting was an exam that she absolutely had to pass. It's not hard to imagine how exhausting this burden of self-doubt was to live with on a daily basis. The sad thing is that this kind of parental anxiety can easily prove contagious – slowly weakening the very connection that this mum was so desperate to preserve.

If this kind of dilemma sounds familiar in any way, you may wish to take a moment to consider some of the following questions:

- Do I worry about whether I'm a good enough role model?

- Do I feel guilty in some way about my performance as a parent – for example, am I afraid that I'm being either too weak or too dictatorial?

- Do I ever worry about what my child thinks of me?

- How effective am I at setting boundaries and sticking to them?

- Does my child ever seem overwhelmed by the choices I am giving them?

- How easy do I find it to say 'no' to my child?

- Do I often question whether I am doing enough to support my child?

I hear parents asking these kinds of questions all the time, and I often wonder: why are we so hard on ourselves? Perhaps it has something to do with the many voices at work in the back of our minds as we bring up our children. When we start our journey as parents, we are never alone. Friends, family, teachers and health professionals all offer well-intentioned advice on the choices we should make and tips for dealing with our child's inevitable growing pains. Aside from this avalanche of advice, there is another influence at work that may have a far bigger impact than even those closest to us: the parenting script we acquired during our own childhood.

All of us have absorbed ideas about what it means to be a mum or dad from the way we were brought up. When we have children, these ideas may influence our own parenting style without us even realizing it. We can easily find ourselves reacting in ways that are reminiscent of our own parents – especially when we are feeling pressured, or facing a situation similar to something that happened in our own early life.

Of course, many of the positive values we've inherited have uplifted us and enriched our own family's lives. But there are times when running on our default setting does not serve us and we may find ourselves reacting in unhelpful ways. This is the moment to step back and consult what I call the 'inner parent' – a source of innate wisdom that we all carry within. This is the part of us that knows how to respond in any given moment – if we can take a moment to pause and listen. By tapping into this guidance, we feel more confident and can respond to the challenges we face every day as parents in new, more creative ways.

The 'inner parent': trusting your instincts

In most areas of our lives, there are clear rules to follow: at school, at work, in social situations, in driving our cars and in the payment of our taxes. The same does not hold true for raising children. Many books offer parents strategies, techniques and step-by-step guides, and you may find they contain valuable tools that work for you and your child. However, the ultimate authority on your daughter or son is you – and the goal of this book is to encourage you to cultivate your own guidance. With a little practice, we can all learn to tune in to the voice of the 'inner parent'. Although we may sometimes forget to consult it, the voice never gives up on us – and over time it will be easier to hear whenever we stop and take five deep breaths, pause, quieten our mind and listen.

Most of us have had an experience of instinctively knowing that something was the right thing to do without necessarily being able to explain why. We might call it an 'intuition' or a 'flash' of insight – knowledge delivered to us from beyond our day-to-day thinking mind. Almost by definition, these are unusual occurrences and most of us don't experience them on any consistent basis. All too often, these messages from our 'inner parent' are drowned out by all the distractions of modern life and of course, that ever-present 'frenemy' who chips away at us and undermines our confidence. It can therefore be a little irritating when somebody says just 'follow your gut' or 'trust your instincts' as if it were as easy as reading an email or opening a letter.

On the other hand, we may have a strong instinct that something's not right – but our 'frenemy' mind starts to question what our intuition is telling us and we end up going around in circles. It's not always easy to hear what our 'inner parent' is saying. But there is an emerging body of scientific research that suggests our intuition is far from 'all in the mind'.

Brain, heart and gut

As we've seen, for most of us, our attention is so caught up in the stream of thinking in our head that we don't pay much attention to what our body is telling us. But researchers are gradually coming round to the idea that listening to our 'gut feelings' or 'following our heart' has a much firmer basis in biology than we might assume.

Scientists used to think that the major organs were controlled by the brain – viewed as a kind of central computer sending instructions to the body below. We now know that things are a lot more complicated than that. Both the gut and the heart have their own 'little brains' – intricate networks of neurons, neurotransmitters, proteins and support cells similar to those found in the brain proper, but functioning largely independently. Indeed, research by the HeartMath Institute in California has shown that the heart produces an electromagnetic field a hundred times more powerful than that of the brain. The field radiates outside the body three feet in every direction and seems to influence other people, even our pets.

The Vagus – the nerve that starts at the base of the skull and meanders through our body – may also play a bigger role in our decision-making than we might imagine. Researchers have discovered that 80 per cent of the Vagus's bandwidth is taken up carrying signals from the body *to* the brain. In a very real sense, we are constantly being fed information by our gut and heart, and these signals seem to play a very significant role in how we think, feel and react.

*

Louise: 'I started listening to myself more'

'When you first have a child, you have no idea what you are doing. Being a mum wasn't instinctive, or intuitive and didn't come naturally to me. I felt like a failure, disempowered and helpless most of the time. I questioned everything I was doing very early on with my daughter, and I just wanted someone to tell me what to do – to give me concrete answers. Although Dr Google and advice from friends and family were helpful at times, sometimes all this information made me doubt myself even more. If you're already a little under-confident, then parenting can play into all those existing insecurities. The parenting industry also dishes out so much fear and anxiety to parents.

'In the end, I got post-natal depression and a lot of anxiety from all the conflicting advice I was reading in books. Everyone seems to tell you something different. People were always trying to make me feel a bit better, and would say to look on the bright side, which only made me feel worse. I had done very well in my job and was always super-organized. Once I had my daughter, everything felt so out of control.

'Fast forward a few years: I am now well again. My home basically looks like a bomb has hit it, but I've learned to be okay with that. What changed? Well, I started listening to myself more, and tapped into my intuition. I found that I had an inner voice guiding me all along.'

Listening to the wisdom of the body

In modern society, we are so dominated by the thought-chatter in our heads that it's easy to lose touch with the heart and the gut altogether – except when they start to hurt. By taking five deep breaths, we turn down the volume of the thoughts that usually absorb almost all of our attention. Every time we create a little gap in the stream of habitual thinking in this way, we make space for intuition to speak silently. It's like a glass of muddy water: clarity appears when the sediment is allowed to settle.

To consult your 'inner parent', it can help to pose your question or request guidance silently or out loud – but don't expect an immediate answer. The response may take time to come. The right choice, answer or guidance will arise far more easily if you are feeling calm than if you are caught up in your busy mind. There is a saying in Tibetan Buddhism: 'First thought – best thought.' This phrase is meant to cut through our tendency to rationalize, weigh up the pros and cons and over-analyse, when our intuition can provide a fresh insight in no time at all.

Try It: Listening to your gut

If you're struggling to make up your mind about something, then the following steps can help you tune in to your gut feeling or instinct:

● Sit comfortably, close your eyes, take five deep breaths and bring the decision you are facing to mind.

● Ask yourself, *'What do I really want in this situation?'* Reflect for a few moments.

● Imagine that you have chosen one of the possible options. Silently say to yourself, *'I have decided to do* [insert decision]. *My mind is made up.'*

● As you hold this choice vividly in your mind, notice how you feel in your body. Pay particular attention to your heart area and your gut, and how you are breathing. Take a few moments to feel the sensation as deeply as you can.

Continued . . .

● Take a few breaths and let the decision go. Allow yourself to relax, and perhaps get up and do something else for a few minutes, or go for a walk.

● Sit down and repeat the exercise, but this time say to yourself, *'No, I'm going to do that instead. I've made up my mind to go with* [insert opposite decision].' Again, imagine this option as vividly as possible, noticing any physical sensations in your body and how you are breathing. Listen to what your body is telling you.

People tend to report generally pleasant feelings when they are contemplating the 'right' decision. Something that doesn't feel like a 'yes' tends to have the opposite effect – there may be tightness in the chest, pressure in the stomach or some other form of discomfort.

Our body helps us to *feel* our thinking and sends constant feedback as to whether we are acting for our highest good – provided we can slow down enough to listen. If we take time to tune in to this feedback, we are less likely to second-guess ourselves and we will feel more confident in our judgement.

As parents, what do we value?

Our culture tends to place a great deal of emphasis on goals – specific things we want to do, be or have in the future. We don't tend to reflect so much on our values – the qualities we want to embody as we go about our daily lives. Goals might be our destination, but values are all about the way we make the journey. For example, one parent may see discipline, order and achievement as very important. Another may place more emphasis on a sense of adventure, laughter and freedom.

Working out the values we prize most highly can take a little work.

From our earliest childhood, all of us have absorbed values from other people: our parents, relatives, teachers, our communities and the media. But there comes a time when we might want to explore what's most important to *us*, rather than following the norms we internalized without question as we grew up. Reflecting on the values you hold most dear is a sure-fire way to build a closer relationship with your 'inner parent' and ensure you are being true to yourself.

This is not just an academic exercise. Making an effort to identify our values and starting to live more in alignment with them can help our experience as parents to unfold with greater harmony. To take a simple example, if one of your most important values is spending time with family, yet you are devoting seventy hours a week to a demanding job, then you are likely to feel constantly stressed. Equally, if you place a high value on connecting with nature and recognize the pleasure it brings you, but you rarely make it out to the countryside, you won't feel your best. Exploring your values helps you to make better decisions – and to be clearer about the kinds of qualities you want to encourage in your children.

I find investigating values is one of the most fruitful avenues in my work with parents. No matter what has happened in the past, it's always possible to get clear in your mind what's important to you now. You can then begin to take small steps towards embodying your values more fully – and feel more confident as a result.

Let's try it now. There's some inspiration in the words overleaf. Scan through them quickly and pick out the first three that leap out at you:

independence **curiosity** **adventure** enthusiasm

humour playfulness **respect**

courage **authenticity** **integrity** knowledge

honesty **creativity** appreciation

diversity order **discipline** nature vitality

collaboration spirituality **beauty** *sensuality*

humility **achievement** intimacy community

resilience fairness **freedom** compassion

forgiveness open-mindedness **tolerance**

romance expression **generosity**

financial security cooperation *gratitude*

When you've settled on your top three values, have a think about how far they are present in your day-to-day life as a parent. For example, let's say you chose the words 'cooperation', 'collaboration' and 'community'. Try to think of some recent examples of how you felt you were cooperating with other parents, or contributing to a community, such as your child's school. It can be really life-affirming to acknowledge the extent to which you are already living these values – perhaps in ways you hadn't really acknowledged before. Equally, you may feel you could be expressing your chosen values more fully. In the case of 'collaboration', perhaps you're keen to forge a closer approach to parenting with your partner. As you reflect on your relationship with your values, it might help to consider some of the following questions:

● What kinds of actions could you take or activities could you pursue that would bring more of these qualities into your everyday experience?

● How much time and energy are you devoting to cultivating your values? What changes could you make? Think about how your values are present in specific areas: family life, relationships, work and leisure.

● Have a discussion with your family about your family's 'core values'.

● Encourage your partner and family members to make their own lists.

● Consider how your list may have been different ten years ago.

● Think about ways in which you'd like to foster your values in the way you interact with your child.

Jo: 'I can't change my son – but I can change how I treat myself'

'You feel like you should be enjoying these years, but my fourteen-year-old, Jamie, is just such a nightmare sometimes. I wish he would show me some appreciation, but I wonder if I'm being needy and my expectations are maybe too high. My mother always told me life isn't fair – and I've grown up to see she was right. I just want to find a way to enjoy life a bit more again without all the battles and stress.'

We talk about Jo's values and come up with:

● **Appreciation.** *'If I was appreciated, Jamie would say thank you for everything I do for him. As it stands, I don't feel like he has any idea about the sacrifices I've made.'*

Continued . . .

● **Humour.** *'We don't have a laugh any more – it's all about having to discipline Jamie. He's always being rude and complaining. I could just do with a giggle with girlfriends – a little light relief from all the tension.'*

● **Fairness.** *'For me, it's about things feeling equal – some give and take. At the moment I feel like I'm drained from just giving – it doesn't feel fair. But I know I shouldn't resent looking after my own son.'*

We talk about what seems to be getting in the way of Jo expressing these values in her daily life: *'If I'm honest, although I want Jamie to say "thank you", I probably don't express that clearly – I mainly just shout. I find it difficult to spell out what I want. It doesn't come naturally to me to speak up because I've always been so busy looking after everyone else. There doesn't seem to be any time to just have fun.'*

Jo and I discuss the kinds of small, deliberate steps she could take to start embodying her values in daily life, rather than looking for them from her son.

● **Appreciation.** *'I'm beginning to see that I could start to show more appreciation for myself, rather than waiting for affirmation from outside. I could start a gratitude journal and use it to check in with myself to see what's gone well each day and how I've handled situations. If I could make this into a habit, it would remind me to appreciate myself more, rather than always waiting for validation and "thank-you"s from others.'*

● **Humour.** *'I could get myself one of the comedy box sets I really used to love. I can't remember the last time I hugged my son or sat down together to watch something funny on TV. He seems so grown up now, but I know he's not too old to enjoy a laugh with his mum.'*

● **Fairness.** *'Fairness is about people treating me properly. I've realized I need to look at my boundaries. If I'm honest, I've always* *been a bit of a doormat. I tend to say "yes" to everything and then end up feeling resentful. Maybe I could come to an agreement with Jamie to share some of the housework.'*

Jo says, 'I know I can't change my son overnight – but I can change the way I treat myself.'

When our buttons are being pushed – and what we can learn from it

As any parent knows, children are experts at pressing our buttons. It's almost as if they arrive pre-programmed to get a reaction out of us, and will keep going relentlessly or refuse to do what they're told until we either give in to their demands or lose our temper. In an instant, we go from being clear-headed and rational to becoming agitated, anxious or angry, or feeling sensitive and upset. You may hear yourself snapping or shouting at them without even knowing where the harsh words came from, or why you are suddenly boiling over. In these flashpoints, any hope of taking a pause to consult your 'inner parent' goes out of the window. When you've had time to calm down, you may see on a logical level that your reaction was out of proportion, but at the time it was impossible to keep your emotions under control.

Becca: 'My daughter's always slagging me off'

'From the moment I open my eyes, my eight-year-old, Jasmine, starts having a go at me. I'm a single parent and she likes to say, "No one will ever want you" and points out my grey hairs. Jasmine's very critical of me. At the swimming pool, I told her to stop pulling our clothes bag

Continued . . .

around, and then everything fell out all over the place. She said, "It's your f—ing fault," and we had a major meltdown there and then. Once, when we were having an argument, Jasmine looked at me and made a gesture as if pulling string out of her ears. I asked what she was doing and she said, "I'm pulling all my happy memories of us out of my brain." I felt shocked and genuinely hurt that my daughter could say such a thing. If you're feeling buoyant then it's okay, and somehow you can excuse things like this. But when you're feeling fairly low it's horrible to have to listen to it. I just don't know what's going on with her.'

Such strong reactions can be a sign that something from our past is playing out in the here and now. The key is to start to see these moments as opportunities to learn more about ourselves, rather than as yet more reasons to beat ourselves up. We begin to approach such flashpoints with curiosity, pausing to investigate what is happening inside our bodies and minds, rather than trying to push our thoughts and sensations away. As we feel our frustration rising, we maintain an awareness of what we're thinking and feeling. As we learn to observe our reactions in the moment – as they are occurring – they begin to lose their power.

As we become more familiar with the feelings that spring from the messier side of parenting, it can help to cast our minds back to reflect a little on what went on during our own childhoods. Whether we remember it fondly or otherwise, our own upbringing will inevitably have shaped our approach to parenting. We may be grateful for what we've learned, or we may want to avoid repeating our parents' mistakes – or a bit of both. Many of us can recognize our own mum's or dad's habitual phrases in the ventriloquist's voice of our 'inner critic' when it says things like, 'There you go, messing things up again!' or 'Why couldn't you have tried just a bit harder?' After telling off our children, we might catch ourselves thinking, 'I sound just like my mum.'

Parents I work with can often be quite surprised when they suddenly realize quite how much their upbringing has shaped their reactions to the challenges they encounter while raising their own kids. You might also be able to see a clear link between episodes from your own childhood and your present parenting style. If you want to look into this more deeply, try scanning the following list of statements to see if any of them remind you of your own early life:

- We didn't talk about feelings in our house.

- It was rare to show affection through touching or hugs.

- We always made sure we sat down together at mealtimes.

- We didn't do conflict and we were always polite.

- The only way to get noticed was by shouting or door-slamming.

- Crying was seen as a weakness.

- Our parents often showed their appreciation for one another.

- Education was a priority; it was all about good grades.

- We often talked about feelings in an open way.

- We felt controlled regarding our choices in education or in our careers.

- Everyone's voice was heard.

- We were allowed to do whatever we wanted with few limits.

- Our parents were always too busy to pay us much attention.

- Mum/Dad made all the decisions and there were no arguments.

- Our parents were always arguing.

- Mum/Dad always insisted everything was great – even if it wasn't.

*

Parental Voices

- James, a dad of three: *'Looking back, my mum was often depressed and she was constantly criticizing herself and everyone around her. She found it very difficult to be optimistic, and tended to have a very gloomy view of the world. She was a "glass half empty" type of person. I can easily find myself slipping into being very negative and I always seem to be beating myself up about my performance as a parent.'*

- Pippa, a mum of two: *'I pride myself on being generally a "together", smart and sensible mum, but there are times when I just seem to lose the plot and start yelling when my son and daughter start playing up – when they don't want to do their homework or are generally being uncooperative. For the longest time, I couldn't understand what was happening – until one day it hit me: "I sound just like my mother." I remember how my own mum used to go ballistic at me and my brothers, and then there'd be hell to pay when Dad finally got home from work. Sometimes we'd get a slap.'*

- Mike, a dad of one: *'I remember my dad as being very harsh and angry and he often drank too much. He used to come in and shout at everyone. I guess it's fair to say I grew up as a worrier. I can see my son is also quite anxious and I can't help blaming myself.'*

We can't change the past, but we can learn to spot when we're reacting in ways that echo how our parents treated us – and themselves. Our early experiences have such a strong impact that it's not always easy to be objective about them and they can easily drown out what our 'inner parent' might be trying to tell us. But if we can start to remember to pause, take five deep breaths and choose our response – rather than acting on autopilot – we'll feel more in control.

If you want to take a closer look at how your parental voices may still be active, it might help to consider some common triggers and responses:

Parental challenge in the present	How the challenge reminds me of my own childhood	How the challenge makes me feel now	What happens when I react without thinking
My kids are squabbling.	My parents used to argue all the time.	Tense; as if I'm about to explode with anger.	I shut down emotionally and withdraw.
My teenage son ignores me and keeps texting as I'm talking.	I often felt ignored as a child and that my parents weren't interested in me.	Rejected and sad; a sinking feeling in my stomach.	I get upset and start shouting to get my son's attention.
My daughter refuses to do what she's told.	My dad was strict and gave me very little freedom as a teenager.	Angry and overwhelmed; a tightness in my chest.	I shout and scream, then slam the door behind me.
My son throws a tantrum in the supermarket and won't stop screaming.	I never felt like I fitted in at school and always worried about being judged.	Anxious and embarrassed; fear of being seen as a bad parent.	I give in to my son's demands because I'm worried about what others think of me.

*

Mo: 'I'm now learning that I'm an adult'

'My own mum's voice is so ingrained in me that for years I made parenting decisions based on what I imagined she would say. Her voice in my head says things like, "If you do it in that way . . . Or if you did it like this . . . then it would be so much better for their education."

'Even though I'm a fully grown adult, I still feel I have to justify things in terms of what my mother would think. But as the years have gone by, I have come to realize that my mum's values are at odds with my own. I have to trust that I have my own set of values and my own way of doing things – and although my decisions may not always be right, I have to make my own mistakes and learn from them.'

Mo and I discuss the concept of 'mistakes'. It's easy with hindsight to look back and think you should have done something differently. But so much of the time we only truly change when things seem to go wrong in some way. So are our mistakes really mistakes – or opportunities to learn?

'I have a constant battle inside myself,' Mo says. 'Do I follow what she says? Or do I break free from the imprint of my mum's voice? I have listened to it a lot over the course of my life, but it's a new thing for me to be so aware of it. Now, when I hear her voice, I say, "That's my mum's voice; it's not mine." The more aware I am, the greater the choice I have over whether to follow it or not. I now realize that my mum doesn't always know best. I tell myself, "Be strong in what you think and what you believe." I am now learning that I am an adult and I have to take responsibility for the choices I make.

'I see an image of a bookshelf in a library. And I can now shelve the thoughts that belong to my mum. I thank her. If I want I can go back to the book with her thought in it and ask myself, is that helpful? Or does it make me doubt myself? What is right for me? What is right for my family?

'I realize now there isn't a "right" thing. It is listening to my intuition that is important. I make my own decisions now – and they're for me, not for Mum, or anybody else.'

Building resilience: allowing your child some bumps

In my work, I see countless young people who lack any confidence in their ability to pick themselves up from a fall, and who are paralysed by a fear of trying new things in case they make a mistake. They feel they can't cope, they worry about the future and they're scared of letting their parents down. The many pressures these young people face – from mounting academic demands to the uncertainties of gaining access to higher education, jobs and homes – are very real. But it's these very pressures that make it more important than ever that our children acquire the resilience they need to navigate the challenges of adolescence and adulthood. They can only do this if they are allowed to make mistakes and fail sometimes.

This can be a difficult process for parents to watch. Mums and dads tell me they are often taken aback by the intensity of the protective instinct that kicked in when they had children. This is only natural: the overwhelming urge to protect our young is a product of millions of years of evolution – it's what's kept the human race going. We all know that falling and picking yourself up again is an essential part of growing up, but the 'parent alarm' can be so sensitive that it can make it extremely hard to watch your child struggle, even for a moment. How do we get the balance right? There are no fixed answers, but allowing a child to overcome challenges in a safe, contained way is essential to help them build their confidence and their life skills – and it sends a powerful message that you trust them.

Whether it's tripping over in the playground, working through conflicts with friends or coping with the death of a much-loved pet, the experience of overcoming adversity is essential to shaping a child's fast-developing brain. As the Canadian psychologist Gordon Neufeld argues, kids *need* sometimes to experience setbacks, sadness and disappointment, otherwise they won't learn to cope with their vulnerable feelings and they will find it difficult to function as independent adults.

Watching your child struggle is never easy. The key is to observe yourself closely and with curiosity to see what comes up for you when your son or daughter is having a hard time. Perhaps you feel a sense of failure and disappointment if your child didn't get the test results they wanted. You may feel angry if your teenager has been caught cyber-bullying another child. Or you may feel an intense sadness when your daughter's friends are giving her the silent treatment. It's no wonder we're often tempted to wade in on their behalf.

Nevertheless, the more you can resist the impulse to react immediately to your own difficult feelings, the more you will be able to soothe your child's temporary distress. Creating a space where you can allow your child's anger, sadness or frustration and help them figure out what action to take for themselves is far more valuable than rushing in to try to fix everything for them. Of course, there are times when it is necessary to intervene to keep a child safe – but kids are a lot tougher than we might think. There is a core of resilience in every young person – but they can only unearth it and learn to trust themselves if they are sometimes allowed to face disappointment, boredom or not getting what they want. Consult your 'inner parent': perhaps what seems like a setback for your child is actually a great opportunity for them to learn and grow.

Cultivating a 'growth mindset'

In the 1990s, the conventional wisdom among psychologists in the 'self-esteem movement' was that the best thing parents could do to help their children was to reinforce their positive self-image by telling them how clever, talented or artistic they were. More recent research suggests that this approach can backfire because children can internalize a fixed idea of themselves that can leave them more vulnerable when things don't turn out the way they had hoped. Children who are constantly told that they are super-intelligent or better than others can become so paralysed by a fear of failure that they struggle to get started or complete tasks. There's a world of difference between a healthy commitment to high standards and the kind of relentless perfectionism that means children put themselves under so much pressure that they can't cope when they achieve anything less than an A*. Children whose self-worth is dependent on success and achievement often live with a harsh 'inner critic' that deters them from trying new things. We can all help our children learn to become more confident if we start to redefine our own idea of success. Rather than focusing purely on external markers of achievement, perhaps we can think more in terms of the unique contribution we can each make to the world and each other.

We need to help young people move away from all-or-nothing thinking and look at situations more flexibly. Our children will be far better equipped to cope with life's untidy realities if they can say to themselves, 'I'd *like* to do well at English' rather than 'I *must* get an A* and anything less would be a disaster.' They can then learn to see 'mistakes' or 'failures' as opportunities to learn and grow rather than as evidence of some inherent flaw that needs to be corrected. Young people will value themselves more if we focus on praising the effort they make rather than the end result. With this in mind, you might wish to use these kinds of phrases when encouraging your children:

- 'I can see that you're trying hard.'

- 'I know it didn't work out this time, but the main thing is the effort you made.'

- 'I admire the way you [add example of something your child does well].'

Psychologists have demonstrated the benefits of this approach. Professor Carol Dweck and fellow researchers at Stanford University have found that students praised for their intelligence tended to choose easier tasks within their comfort zone, apparently fearing the consequences of failure. Those praised for their effort, by contrast, chose to work on problems that would stretch their abilities. The researchers described the two approaches in terms of 'mindsets':

- **Fixed mindset.** Kids who were constantly told they were smart or successful viewed intelligence as a fixed quantity that they either did or didn't possess. They worried about *proving* their ability rather than improving, and were less likely to take on difficult problems and more likely to get upset if they failed.

- **Growth mindset.** Kids who were taught that intelligence is a malleable quality that can be increased with effort and learning tended to have more constructive thoughts and were more flexible about changing their strategy if what they were doing wasn't working.

These differences were reflected in brain activity. For example, after being given the solution to a test question they had answered incorrectly, students with a 'growth mindset' displayed greater activation of brain regions associated with the deep processing of language – suggesting that they were confronting their mistake and trying to learn from it. Indeed, activation in this brain region predicted better performance in a later test.

The way you give praise can help to cultivate a 'growth mindset'. For example, when a child seeking approval shows you a piece of work, look for specific details to praise, rather than making generalizations about how talented they are. For example, 'I love the colours in this picture' rather than 'You're such a great artist.'

Another sure way to help your child cultivate a 'growth mindset' is to help them spend as much time as possible outdoors. Exploring nature, with all its rugged obstacles, is an excellent way to provide them with opportunities to learn to assess risk and problem-solve for themselves.

Ayesha: 'They're learning valuable lessons'

'My ten-year-old, Arshad, was saying, "I'm bored!" I screamed, "You can just be bored then!" I felt bad. I felt like I should be trying to make everything okay for him. But I can't. I'm so tired and I feel like I'm at my limit. But you just want to make it all all right for them, don't you? You want to make everything okay.

'Later, in the playground, I saw another boy being mean to my son. All these strong emotions came to the surface, and I felt a surge of anger towards that other child. I wanted to throttle him. That instinct to protect my child is so strong that I could never have imagined how difficult it would be to override those angry feelings and not react immediately.

'But I know the reality is that I'm not doing Arshad any favours in the long term. The reality is that my son will have to learn to manage his own friendships and be disappointed sometimes – even though I'm his greatest supporter, and I'll always be there for him. And sometimes he'll just have to learn to amuse himself like we used to – I can't constantly keep coming up with new, exciting things for him to do. He needs to learn that there can't always be an adult to entertain him, and that he'll still be okay.'

No such thing as perfect

Every mum and dad wants to do the best they can, and it's easy to blame ourselves when we feel we're not getting it 'right'. But there's no such thing as perfect when it comes to parenting. We learn the most during the challenges and the hard times – when we fall down and pick ourselves up. As we gradually become more comfortable with the inevitable messiness, we survive the lows and relish the highs. This is the journey that makes us stronger and wiser, and teaches us that our children are here to help us learn the greatest lesson of all: to trust ourselves.

*

The five key points

Getting to know your 'inner parent'

- You are the ultimate authority on your kids: trust your 'inner parent'.

- Explore how your childhood has shaped your parenting style.

- We can choose to parent in line with our own values.

- Allow your child some bumps: it's the only way to build resilience.

- Every parent is doing their best: there's no such thing as perfect.

Part II
You and Your Child

Session 6

A deeper connection

There are times when parents experience a profound sense of connection with their child – a priceless bond they could not imagine sacrificing for anything. But there can also be moments when your child's constant demands for attention are so exhausting that you wonder how you'll cope. A gulf seems to open and any sense of harmony vanishes in the midst of arguments, tantrums, angry exchanges or sulking. Drained by your child's behaviour, and desperate to make them behave at any cost, it's easy to resort to threats or bribes. When these backfire, your son or daughter only becomes more argumentative or withdrawn. It feels as if something infinitely precious has been lost – and it's easy to worry that you won't get it back.

Restoring, nurturing and strengthening a HEART-centred connection is the subject of the rest of this book. However wide the gap may seem, there's always a way to build a bridge – if you can begin to respond to familiar situations in new ways. Mindfulness helps us to see when we're slipping into our old reactions, to pause and choose again. Gradually, the HEART-qualities we explored in the first half of the book – Humility,

Empathy, Authenticity, Respect and Trust – become touchstones in our daily interactions. The moment-to-moment work of meeting our feelings with curiosity, and cultivating kindness for ourselves and others, starts to bear fruit.

Sarah: 'I learned to reconnect with my daughter'

When Sarah came to see me she was desperate. She had always enjoyed a warm relationship with her daughter, Anne-Marie, who had just turned thirteen. But something had changed. Anne-Marie would come home late from school, refuse to eat dinner and slam doors, then retreat to her room and spend hours on Snapchat. When Sarah tried to speak to her, Anne-Marie would fold her arms and roll her eyes. Sarah told me, *'I don't know where my little girl's gone.'*

When Sarah reflected on Anne-Marie's behaviour, wondering what was underlying her acting-up, she started to recognize that her own anxiety and preoccupation with her new boyfriend had distracted her from giving her daughter the attention and HEART-centred connection she desperately needed.

When Sarah was able to find the calm place within herself and share how she was feeling with Anne-Marie, her daughter surprised her by telling her that she felt bad for letting her down. Sarah, in turn, apologized – providing for her daughter a model of how to admit a mistake. This encouraged Anne-Marie to acknowledge the upset she'd caused to her mother.

By taking time to really listen to one another, they were able to agree to set aside ten to fifteen minutes after school each day when, over a relaxing cup of coffee, Sarah could ask Anne-Marie how her day had gone – if she felt like sharing. The two of them recently spent a Sunday baking together – a sure sign that their connection was getting stronger again.

The art of listening

Though I suffered my share of setbacks when I was growing up, I was fortunate in one crucial respect: my grandmother, Marguerite, was an expert listener. Every evening when she was cooking dinner at our bungalow, she would ask me how my day had gone at school. She always resisted the urge to impose solutions on me when I was struggling, though I now recognize how great the temptation must have been. My grandmother modelled the kind of attentive, non-judgemental listening that I now do my best to explore in my work with parents.

When a child comes to you with a problem – whether it be friends, school or an argument with a sibling – it's natural to want to suggest solutions born of your own much longer life experience. We may instinctively offer advice, perhaps in the way our own parents did when we were upset. Of course, there may be situations where we need to take action as a result of what our child is telling us – particularly if we feel they are at risk in some way. We may even be desperate to ensure our child doesn't repeat mistakes we feel we've made in our lives.

Nevertheless, sometimes we would do better to hold back on the impulse to offer solutions. There will be many times when all your child really wants is someone to empathize with and validate what they're experiencing; they aren't necessarily asking you to make things better or make things go away. Often, the best thing a parent can do is to provide a safe space where their child can be open and honest about how they are feeling. By being there for them in this way, you can help them to learn to face their fears and appreciate the comforting truth that even the most troubling emotions eventually subside, no matter how scary they might at first seem.

To adult ears, a lot of what preoccupies children can seem trivial – or even boring – compared to 'real' problems. But it's important to remember that the distress a child experiences when worrying about something that is going on in their life is no different to the anxiety we might get when preoccupied with grown-up concerns. Indeed, if we are too quick to jump in and offer 'fixes', a child may feel that we haven't really understood the depth of the anxiety and hurt they're going through. Equally, when we take time to listen to our child, we may be surprised to discover that they see a situation very differently to us, and that we've made assumptions about what they're thinking without checking whether they are correct.

You'll have more headspace to focus on your child's concerns if you've been able to find a chance to offload yourself, whether it be with your partner, family or friends. All parents go through crises or difficulties, including in relationships, health and work, and it's not a weakness to admit that you need some extra help. Even writing down how you are feeling can provide a temporary relief, and you can always use the journal at the end of this book (page 259).

Annie: 'Listening carefully was enough'

'With my kids, I often find myself trying to solve things and find all the answers. But I'm starting to realize the power of just listening, rather than jumping in with a solution.

'The other day, my children were watching a film and they seemed to really be enjoying it. I went through to the kitchen to prepare dinner, and about twenty minutes later my six-year-old son came through in floods of tears. I couldn't work out what was wrong and he said, "The man in the film never got any food." My son got on my knee, and he had to sit and talk about it. Just talking through it, just being empathized with, made him feel much better. Of course, it was only a kids' film, but it was something that in that moment was really important to him. I realized I didn't have to offer any answers. Just being with him and listening carefully was enough.'

Sometimes your child may tell you a story about how they think things unfolded that you know does not correspond to the facts. It's worth bearing in mind that this is their perspective on what happened, and it's important to challenge them as respectfully as possible – validating their feelings, if not their interpretation of events. Of course, there is a role for offering solutions or problem-solving. But the act of listening attentively can be a vital first step and much more powerful than any advice we may give. We've all had the experience of wanting to get something off our chest without being judged. Perhaps this act of deep, focused attention will provide an opportunity for your child to reach out for parental guidance, something they may have resisted in the past, or even open a door that will enable them to find a solution for themselves.

On the other hand, you may find yourself in a situation where you feel your child has a legitimate concern but you are stuck for what to suggest. That's okay too: children understand that just because you are an adult, it doesn't mean you have all the answers. You're not disappointing them – they can accept that you don't know everything. Being honest with your child is a vital part of a HEART-centred connection because it makes them feel respected. The most important thing is not necessarily coming up with a solution: it's allowing your child to be truly heard.

Like any skill, the art of listening can be honed with practice. Here are some more suggestions for ways to focus on your child as fully as you can:

- **Five deep breaths.** As you start to listen, become aware of your breathing – and take five deep breaths. This will help you to remain centred and present no matter what may arise in the conversation.

- **Be aware of how you feel in your body.** Keep some attention in your body: notice how your hands feel as they rest in your lap, or the feeling of your feet on the floor. This will help you stay anchored in the here and now.

- **Phone and devices out of the way.** It's obviously important to avoid answering the phone or texting during a conversation – but it's also good to go a step further and ensure the phone is kept out of sight in a bag or pocket and switched into silent mode. Turn off the TV or radio.

● **Active listening.** Reflect back what a child says to you, showing you're empathizing with them and validating their experience. For example, you might say something like, 'So, you're saying you feel sad/frustrated right now?' or 'That must be hard for you.' This is part of an approach called 'active listening' taught by the psychologist Carl Rogers, in which you repeat or paraphrase what you've heard and gently seek clarification if necessary.

● **Avoid interruptions or the temptation to finish another's sentence.** Children can quickly shut down or edit their responses if they don't feel heard. If you do find yourself jumping in – which is normal – take a moment to say you're sorry for interrupting, and go back to active listening.

● **Notice body language – your own as well as your child's.** Ensure your body language is open and friendly, rather than hunched or defensive. You can immediately strike a more receptive pose by uncrossing your arms or legs. If a younger child is on the floor, you might want to get down to their level, or offer a hug or other form of friendly touch if this feels right.

● **Care with words.** Just as we can be more mindful of what our child is saying, so we can choose our own words more carefully. We can pause before responding, notice the effects our words are having and sometimes choose to remain silent if we can't find the right thing to say. Of course, it's natural to feel upset when our child is distressed. It's hard not to get caught up in their anger, sadness or frustration, and before we know it we've said or done something we later regret. But, little by little, it is possible to learn to pause, take a step back and think through your response.

Try It: Mindful listening

The next time you are talking with your child, see if you can use it as an opportunity to practise mindful listening. Offering another person our full attention is one of the most precious gifts we can give:

● Can you sit, for five minutes, just listening, without coming up with a solution?

● Can you bring more focus to the sound of your child's voice, their body language and their facial expression?

● Pay attention to any thoughts and sensations that arise. Do you feel any boredom, irritation or an urge to jump in? Can you observe these feelings and let them pass?

● Can you keep some of your attention on your breath, or in your body?

Afterwards, take a moment to reflect on how it went. Did you feel any difference in the quality of the conversation? How did you feel about yourself when you made a conscious effort to pay attention in this way? How did your child seem to respond? We may find that the act of listening has a more powerful impact on our child than any attempt to try to solve their problems for them.

*

Naomi: 'I've learned to give advice less and listen more'

'It's so painful to watch my fourteen-year-old daughter, Sophie, struggle with the critical voice in her head. I realize I want to fix things for her because I have exactly the same 'inner critic' myself – she must have inherited it from me. I keep telling her how amazing she is, but she can't seem to hear it. I can see exactly what she needs to do and I want so much to help her because she seems so unhappy and vulnerable. But she never takes any of my advice on board. I keep trying, but nothing I say seems to help.'

I ask Naomi to imagine what kind of feelings would come up for her if she simply listened to Sophie rather than immediately offering advice. Naomi knows she would feel very uncomfortable: even hearing her daughter pouring out her troubles for a few minutes is enough to tie a knot in her stomach. As we discuss this further, Naomi starts to see how her daughter's anxiety triggers a similar anxiety reaction in herself. She remembers all the times in her own life when she's lacked confidence, especially when she was Sophie's age. She realizes that she is a mirror for her daughter's feelings.

As we talk, Naomi starts to reflect on how she interacts with Sophie. She recognizes that she's so anxious to make sure Sophie's okay that she can't resist bombarding her with questions as soon as she gets home from school. Sometimes she catches herself thinking aloud as she tries to understand her daughter, saying things like, 'I think you've got low self-esteem,' or 'I wonder if this is all because your dad's not been around enough?' She does her best to boost her daughter's confidence by telling her how 'amazing' she is and that 'you're beautiful to me'.

Naomi's attempts at reassurance fail to have any impact because Sophie can sense that they are coming from her mum's head, rather than her heart. Sophie simply doesn't feel 'amazing', no matter how many times Naomi tells her how wonderful she is. Sophie doesn't want reassuring *words*; she craves a HEART-centred connection. She wants her mum to show she understands her emotional pain is real, rather than try to talk her out of it because it makes her feel so uncomfortable.

I work with Naomi to remind her to take five deep breaths and remain firmly focused in the present moment whenever she starts to feel anxious. By learning to tolerate her own feelings in this way, she starts to see her anxiety for what it really is: a very unpleasant, yet temporary and fleeting sensation in her stomach. Naomi slowly learns to back off for a moment and give her daughter some space. For the first time, she realizes that there is often no need to say much at all. Through her calm and empathic presence, she offers Sophie far more emotional support than any words can convey.

At first, Naomi's own 'inner critic' kicks in and she begins to beat herself up for being such an 'annoying mum' in the past. But as we continue to work together, she recognizes that allowing her own critical voice to run riot in this way isn't helping her or her daughter. Naomi learns to go easier on herself and let her conversations with Sophie unfold with less advice and more pauses. Sophie senses the trust her mum has in her and has gained greater confidence in her ability to find her own answers as a result.

'It's been amazing to see what a difference it makes when I really listen,' Naomi says. *'It's been hard not to rush in with my ideas about what Sophie should or shouldn't do — but the effort's been worth it. I'm focusing now on offering a steady drip-drip of encouragement when things are going well, rather than giving her big chats about how amazing she is. The funny thing is that she has now actually started asking for my opinion rather than always pushing me away. We are definitely more connected than we were, and that feels good.'*

*

Pets, 'power animals' and imaginary friends

Often one of the first things psychologists do when working with children is to ask them to draw a 'genogram', or family tree. When I was starting out in my career, I would sometimes ask children to include pets, which would go on the diagram in a sibling role. Even in families under the most severe strain, I began to notice that the mere mention of the family cat, dog or hamster would immediately lighten the atmosphere. Over the years, I learned to include this as a routine part of the exercise – and it never fails to make everyone smile.

I have worked with many families where animals have provided a way for children and parents to bond – whether it be through the shared duties of caring for a pet or visiting animals in a sanctuary or urban farm. Animals naturally awaken compassion in children, who can sense they share their own vulnerability. Animals are also the perfect teachers of mindfulness – living in the moment, not worrying about past or future, happy just to be, exactly as they are.

It's great for any child to have a chance to interact with animals, but for those who are experiencing emotional difficulties of any kind, the experience can be particularly powerful. Children are highly sensitive to how they are perceived by their peers and adults; when looking into the eyes of an animal, they can be sure they are never being judged.

The benefits children can derive from bonding with animals can also extend into the realm of their imaginary friends – whether they be human-like boys or girls, or 'power animals' such as bears, horses or big cats, or even mythical dragons, unicorns or fairies. When I was seven, I met an imaginary lion that helped me during difficult times at school. He would walk ahead of me down the street, offer comforting words and provide a strong, reassuring presence. I could vividly feel his aura of kindness and strength, particularly after I lost my mother.

Younger children don't have to be facing difficulties to invent an imaginary friend, nor is their arrival necessarily a sign that a child is feeling awkward or lonely. In fact, children who have imaginary friends often tend to be particularly creative and empathic. Interacting with imaginary friends can be a great way for them to practise seeing things from different perspectives and develop their imagination, as well as being a wonderful source of humour and fun.

Though we tend to associate imaginary friends with young children, some therapists are discovering that 'power animals' can work well for adults. US psychologist Lisa Schwarz, developer of the Comprehensive Resource Model of psychotherapy, leads her clients in a visualization exercise to meet 'power animals' which help them work through their problems. Schwarz and her colleagues believe that working with 'power animals' in this way may strengthen the pathways in the brain that give us a sense of security and being cared for in our human relationships. As adults, it softens our hearts when we can access the imaginary world and recapture some of the childlike elements of ourselves that we may have forgotten somewhere along the way. If you find that you or your young child is sheltering an invisible house guest, here are some tips:

- Acknowledge the being as a legitimate presence in the household. Be curious about it and try not to dismiss it as a figment of a child's imagination.

- Speaking to the imaginary friend may help you understand your child's perspective on certain issues and strengthen your connection with them.

- Avoid any temptation to speak on behalf of the imaginary friend – this is a relationship 'owned' by the child, and they will have the final say on what this unseen visitor is thinking, feeling or doing.

- Trust your 'inner parent'. It's obviously not acceptable for a child to blame bad behaviour on an imaginary friend, use it as an excuse or follow its 'advice' if it's going to lead them into problems. If conflicts arise, you could use the imaginary friend or 'power animal' to help your child problem-solve. For example, you could ask, 'What would your "friend"/"power animal" do?' to help your child with a particular dilemma. This can be a good way to help them learn to explore new perspectives. No matter what happens, your child will feel empowered if you treat their 'friend' with respect and try to enter into their world.

Setting limits

Telling a child what they can and can't do is one of the trickiest parts of any parent's job. So many mums and dads tell me they find it difficult to know where to place boundaries and how to teach their child right from wrong. Everyone can agree that learning to accept the feeling of frustration and disappointment of not getting what you want is an essential part of growing up. It's easy to forget that parents face their own equivalent of this process: learning to work with their own hurt feelings, frustrations and confusion in the face of their child's hostility, rejection or anger. When confronted with a child who is pushing limits, it's easy to be pulled in several directions at once:

- **Our own parental influences.** We can find ourselves automatically resorting to the kind of discipline strategies our own parents may have used on us, regardless of whether they fit with our values or what our 'inner parent' would choose.

- **Voices of our partner, friends or relatives.** We defer to the many people telling us how to parent – with their advice often reflecting the influence of their own parents.

- **Feeling our child's distress.** Our child's upset can reawaken the part within all of us that remembers how we felt as children when we didn't get our own way, or felt our needs were not being met.

The first step towards becoming more comfortable with setting limits is to acknowledge how difficult it can be. The more you can become aware of the competing influences, the more you can step back and take the pause needed to listen to the voice of your 'inner parent' and choose your response in any given moment. There is no fixed answer or universal strategy that will work for all children at all times. You will be in a much better position to know what the situation requires if you're able to take five deep breaths and trust your own judgement.

It helps to remember that children need structure. Some mums and dads fear their child will misinterpret their firmness as a sign of coldness or lack of love. I reassure them that this fear is misplaced: as long as our boundaries spring from a kind and open heart, they will do no harm. Setting limits is not about power and control – it's a vital part of a HEART-centred connection. Kids love confident parents who show leadership, as well as compassion and empathy. They will respond well when you take the time to explain clearly the reasons why you have decided on certain limits, and that you want to work with them to keep them safe.

Even when a child does not understand the reason for a boundary, they will feel more confident when they discover their parents draw clear, consistent lines, no matter how much they might complain and cry, 'It's not *fair*!' It becomes easier to stand our ground when we recognize that a child's attempts to push boundaries are their way of exploring how the world works – and frequently a bid for our attention, even if delivered clumsily and in a way that's more likely to provoke our irritation than our affection.

How you go about setting limits will vary according to the temperament of your child and the way they develop as they get older. If a young child complains and manipulates you to win a reprieve, they may appear momentarily satisfied – but in reality the feeling of being stronger than their parent will make them feel very uneasy. However much they may whine and complain, and say, 'You never let me have my way,' or 'I never get what I want,' a child will respect you in the long run if you stick to your word.

We all want our children to like us, but ultimately our role is not to be their friend, but to be their parent. Children can only feel fully secure when they know where the boundaries lie. Setting rules with clear consequences for breaking them is not about being a dictator: it's an act of love that helps our children learn to navigate the rule-based world outside their home.

Naughtiness or bid for attention?

Children can be at their most exasperating when they seem deliberately to act up or misbehave for no apparent reason. It can be very easy for a despairing parent confronted with a boundary-pushing child to slip into self-blame and wonder if they're doing the right thing. In our frustration, we may even start to think of our child as 'ungrateful', 'difficult' or 'selfish'. However much we may want to, it's not always easy to see our child from the fresh perspective of somebody who is meeting them for the first time.

It's also important to recognize that there will be times when your child is so hard to cope with that you may experience strong feelings of resentment towards them. Many parents I see tell me they feel bad when this happens. I always tell them to go a little easier on themselves. A surge of resentment does not mean you don't love your child – every parent struggles with this and it's normal to go through moments when you just don't like them very much. It's important in these situations to draw a distinction between the child you love and the behaviour you don't like. Try to take a step back and consider what may lie beneath your child's behaviour, rather than focusing on what they are doing wrong.

When your child is trying to get your attention, it's often a bid for a deeper connection – whether they are being 'good' or 'bad'. What can seem like acting up or naughtiness can be a misguided attempt to form the HEART-centred connection they crave. Of course, many factors can drive challenging behaviour, from tiredness and hunger to a bad day at school or tension with a sibling. However, when confronted with a persistent pattern, it may be worth asking whether it's your child's way of saying:

- 'I want you to listen to me.'

- 'I want your attention.'

- 'I want to feel like I'm a worthy person.'

- 'I want to know you love me.'

- 'I want to know that I can trust you to be my place of safety.'

- 'I want some of your time – just you and me, no distractions.'

Rather than reacting immediately, the first step you can take towards defusing the situation is to notice whether your child's behaviour has triggered a spike in your own feelings of anger, frustration or self-blame. This is the moment to take a pause and ask your 'inner parent' what is the right thing to do. There will be time later to address the deeper issues – but it's obviously counter-productive to react in the heat of the moment. It may be that you need to hug your child, leave the room for a short while, or drop down to their level and quietly speak to them. If they're older, it might be time to recognize that you're both getting stressed and press the pause button by asking, 'Do we both need to take a few minutes before we speak again?'

Bringing mindfulness into fraught moments is hard, but it's a skill that develops over time. It can be a real help to practise as much as possible during periods of relative calm – by taking five deep breaths, tuning in to your breathing or performing a quick 'check-in' with your body sensations. This will help ensure you can use these tools even under pressure. Try not to make being 'mindful' another goal to strive towards, but if you do find yourself over-analysing, that's okay too. Just come back to the moment, breathe and begin again. Each moment is a fresh start.

How conflict can bring us closer

Rows, tears, angry words and slammed doors are an inevitable part of any parent–child relationship, but the hurt feelings they cause can linger. As adults, our instinct may be to put the upset behind us as quickly as possible and move on, secure in the knowledge that we've weathered many such storms in the past without any lasting harm. Or we might even feel guilty if we lost our temper or used harsh words and prefer to pretend the whole episode never happened. We may assume that our child's silence means that all has been forgiven. Children and teens don't have the benefit of our experience, however, and their hurt feelings may feel to them as though they will never go away, or their resentment towards us may last longer than we might assume.

As adults, it's up to us to take the lead in repairing these cracks to ensure they don't lead to bigger problems. Everyday tensions and disagreements can build up over time, leading to ever more frequent misunderstandings and pointed fingers. We may be justifiably angry, and feel disrespected by children who seem to be walking all over us or taking us for granted. But by finding the humility to revisit what happened when we're feeling calmer, we can turn the aftermath of conflicts into opportunities to deepen our connection. All relationships need work, and taking these moments to make sure that any outstanding grievance has been aired and resolved is one of the most powerful ways we can strengthen our family's foundations.

Transgender Children

In the past few years, there's been a lot of focus in the media on transgender children: those who identify with the opposite gender to their biological sex. In the past, it was extremely difficult for a child to live openly as transgender, but these days society is starting to become more accepting. As awareness of these issues has increased, so has the number of families seeking professional support. According to a recent report in the *Guardian*, referrals to the Tavistock Gender Identity Development Service for young people have risen sharply since its first year of operation in 1989, when it received only two clients. In 2015, the clinic received 1,400 referrals – double the number of the previous year. Of these 1,400, nearly 300 were under the age of twelve, with some as young as three.

Today's transgender kids – and the parents who raise them – are in many respects pioneers, and have much to teach the rest of us about the value of learning to see the world from new perspectives. However, as a parent it's still normal to feel a sense of shock or confusion at discovering your child may see themselves very differently to how you imagined them. Many parents question whether they may have somehow done something 'wrong', even though they know that being transgender is not a choice: it's just the way a child is. Some parents may grieve or feel a sense of loss for the child they thought they had, worry how others might react, or fear what the future may hold.

No matter what kind of feelings you may experience, it's important to acknowledge and accept them, using the kinds of mindfulness tools discussed in Part I. Whatever your child's particular situation, you can always provide them with a HEART-centred connection. Here are some pointers that some of my parents have found helpful:

● **Take their feelings seriously.** Many young boys and girls may enjoy playing with toys or wearing clothes traditionally associated with the opposite gender – this doesn't make them transgender. However, if a child is consistently certain that they identify with another gender then they need to be taken seriously, even if they are still very young. Have patience: it may take time for their gender identity to become clear.

● **Allow space.** If a child is questioning their gender identity, it's important to allow them to explore – which might mean letting them experiment with different ways of dressing, presenting themselves, or even using different names. A child's gender identity can be fluid, and they need your support, encouragement and above all acceptance as they seek to become more at ease with who they are.

● **Seek support.** It's not always easy to navigate the complexities of gender-identity issues, so it's crucial to seek

Continued . . .

professional advice and avoid imposing self-diagnosed labels. Some young children will grow to be more comfortable in their birth gender, while others may find themselves somewhere on a wide spectrum of possible identities. Finding the right support on this journey can make all the difference. (For more information, see the GIDS website listed on page 249.)

The healing power of laughing – or allowing our tears to flow

Parenting can feel very serious at times, so it's good to allow yourself the odd moment to reconnect with your own light-heartedness and laughter. Becoming more present can help us to rediscover some of the qualities of curiosity, playfulness and imagination that come so naturally to young people but which can easily be overtaken by our commitments as parents. Don't underestimate what every child knows: the power of humour to cut through an argument and lift a heavy atmosphere. We can't be anywhere else than in the moment if we're laughing. Possibilities might include:

- Rough-and-tumble play

- Watching funny videos on YouTube

- Feeding ducks at the local river or pond

- Collecting leaves, acorns or conkers in a park

- Dancing to fun tunes

- Going barefoot

- Dressing-up

- Playing charades or another family game

- Putting on a silly voice

We also need to remember that our bodies are designed to cry. We can probably all recall a time from childhood when allowing ourselves to surrender to our urge to sob brought a profound feeling of relief. There are very real, physiological reasons why letting go in this way can be so healthy. Researchers have discovered that crying tears of sadness helps wash many types of stress hormones out of the system and causes the body to release a natural painkiller called leucine enkephalin.

Yet for all the healing balm that crying offers, adults often struggle to connect to their tears. The US family therapist Susan Stiffelman says she often sees people with what she calls 'dry-eyed syndrome': no matter how intense their sadness or grief, they simply cannot start releasing these feelings by crying. In my experience, the same is often true in Britain. I've had so many parents from all walks of life say to me, 'I know the tears are there, but I just cannot cry.' There often seems to be a fear of the temporary loss of control that tears may bring. We've convinced ourselves that we're fine as long as we're not crying – when crying is the very thing that could make us feel better. One mother said, 'I know I need to cry, but I'm afraid once I start I'll never stop.'

Our resistance to crying can colour our response to the tears of others. How many of us feel uncomfortable when a friend starts to sob and immediately rush in to try to cheer them up? Of course, helping somebody work through their problems is often the right thing to do. But when tears are in full flow, it can be even more powerful to resist the impulse to offer reassurance and meet their sorrow or grief with silent companionship. Far from being a sign of weakness, having the courage to face these feelings – however many tears they evoke – is a mark of strength.

Our tears can also provide a powerful opportunity to deepen our HEART-centred connection with our child. Children, particularly when they are younger, are acutely aware of how they are perceived by their parents and will do almost anything to please them, including squashing their urge to cry. One thirteen-year-old girl would always hold back from the brink of tears, saying, 'I'm all right, I'm all right. My mum wants me to be okay, she doesn't want me to be upset or see me crying.'

She is far from alone. Young boys also need mature masculine role models who can show them that it's not a sign of weakness to show they are sad sometimes. Some kids will lash out in anger precisely because expressing aggression feels safer to them than revealing their vulnerability through tears.

Dealing with grief and loss

When somebody dies, it's perfectly understandable for a parent to try to protect their child by hiding their grief. As a society, we're not particularly good at confronting death and acknowledging that passing away is part of the cycle of life. If we can find the courage to talk about our feelings, we can use our loss as an opportunity to explain that tears are a normal sign of sadness and not something to fear. Children have a higher tolerance for our own upset than we often assume – provided we explain to them what is happening and reassure them that we will be okay, and that they are not to blame. It's much better to model the healthy expression of emotion than pretend that everything's okay.

How do we reconnect with our tears? As we begin to observe our thoughts and feelings with greater clarity, we learn to see more clearly when we are shutting down. As we go more deeply into our sadness, we might notice our 'inner critic' coming up with thoughts such as:

- 'Pull yourself together – these are just First World problems.'

- 'What have you got to complain about?'

- 'Stop being such a baby.'

- 'Why are you making such a fuss?'

- 'Stop! You're over-reacting.'

- 'Don't worry – it's not that bad.'

There is nothing wrong with these voices – they are merely remnants of the kinds of conditioning that we've all received in childhood. The more we can become aware of them operating in us in the here and now, the more we can make contact with our authentic feelings. If this involves some tears, then so be it. Once we are able to step into our own sadness, feel it fully and realize that it will not kill us, then we are in a much better position to provide a safe space for our child to work through their own experiences of loss without feeling they need to hide their pain away.

Learning to forgive our child – and ourselves

However much we may try, it's not always easy to maintain a HEART-centred connection with our child: life has a habit of getting in the way. We can all lose our temper in a way we later regret, and we can all find ourselves giving in to a child's relentless demands at the end of a long day of doing our utmost to maintain firm boundaries. That's why cultivating forgiveness is so important – both for yourself and for your child.

The 'frenemy' in our head is often very reluctant to let us forgive ourselves. But we can perhaps find a moment to show ourselves some compassion. Ask if you can forgive yourself for:

- Losing my temper

- Not saying the right thing

- Resenting my child

- Feeling like a failure

- Comparing myself unfavourably to others

One friend of mine who looks after her children full-time said that at times it can be a lonely and thankless task being a parent; she has accepted that her husband, her own parents and her children will probably never express the kind of appreciation that deep down she would love. Instead, she tries as often as she can to tell herself, 'You're doing really well.' She has recognized and accepted the need to be her own cheerleader. If I were to be granted ten seconds to offer one message to each of the mums and dads I work with, it would be this: even the smallest steps you can take towards being kinder to yourself matter far more than you might imagine.

Try It: Getting in touch with forgiveness

Take a moment to sit quietly – you can do this at home, at work or on the bus. Close your eyes, become aware of your breathing and settle your attention into your body. Take a few moments to check in with yourself, and observe the sensations in your body and the thoughts in your mind.

Then silently repeat the following phrases, or a variation of your choice (perhaps emphasizing self-kindness, happiness or contentment):

● *May I be more forgiving of myself.*

● *May I be more forgiving of my child.*

● *May all parents be more forgiving of themselves.*

● *May I be happy. May my child be happy. May all parents be happy.*

As you repeat this mantra for as long as you wish, see what comes up for you. Do you experience any new thoughts or sensations? Do you feel any different? You can repeat this exercise very briefly at any time of day when you need a little lift.

*

The five key points

A deeper connection

● Mindfulness helps us to find new ways of connecting with our child.

● You don't need all the answers as a parent: sometimes just listening is enough.

● Setting boundaries can be hard, but they make kids feel safe.

● Allow yourself to laugh – and to cry.

● Parenting is messy: learn to forgive yourself and your child.

Session 7

Managing meltdowns

It's a scene that so many parents have learned to dread: your child's face scrunches, tears well and the scream begins – a piercing, nerve-shredding wail that just won't seem to stop. The feeling triggers a reaction in your own body: your heart sinks, your jaw tightens and frustration starts to build. You're already late, but no matter how much you try to cajole, reason with or comfort your child, nothing seems to work. Your own anger begins to simmer in response. 'I hate you so much,' your child shouts – and suddenly you're filled with a feeling of profound hostility towards the very person you love the most.

There can be few greater challenges to maintaining your inner balance than a child's full-blown meltdown. Temper tantrums are one of the most common – and most difficult – problems parents face, often leaving them with a feeling that they cannot 'find their child' underneath all the rage and tears. It's no wonder we can quickly reach boiling point ourselves and end up acting in ways we may later regret. It can be very easy to take your child's behaviour personally and start telling yourself that their moods must be a reflection of your poor parenting skills.

Many of the parents I've seen have relentlessly beaten themselves up because they feel they should be able to manage their children's tantrums without ending up so shouty and stressed. The fact that every mum and dad feels helpless sometimes doesn't make it any easier.

These are the kinds of things I often hear from parents:

- 'Not being able to fix my child's anger makes me feel powerless.'

- 'I feel like strangers are judging me when my child acts up in public.'

- 'I feel embarrassed that I can't seem to control my child.'

- 'If we don't sort this out quickly, the teenage years are going to be even worse.'

- 'I can't understand why she lashes out at the people who love her.'

- 'It's painful to hear someone I love so much being so disrespectful.'

- 'I'm scared of my child when he gets angry.'

- 'I feel so guilty that somehow I did something wrong in the early years, and now he hates me, and all I want is for him to love me.'

These thoughts and feelings are perfectly normal and understandable, but it may help to consider your child's behaviour from a new perspective: the fast-developing field of neuroscience. Though we may belong to a more stressed-out generation than our parents, we also have one big advantage: advances in neuro-imaging mean we know a lot more about how a child's brain develops in their early years. Parents may be quick to blame themselves, but emotional storms gripping a child are often less a symptom of some parental failing than they are the result of a temporary mismatch between the thinking and feeling parts of a young brain. Children have a lot of energy – and that's a wonderful blessing. In this session we look at how to channel it in the healthiest possible ways.

A construction site in the skull

We can all see the very obvious outer changes that occur as a child grows up, but the most important developments happen on the inside. Human brains are comprised of about eighty-six billion neurons – specialized nerve cells that relay information throughout the brain and nervous system. Babies are born with almost all the neurons they will ever have already in place, but the brain itself grows rapidly, doubling in size in the first year and reaching 80 per cent of its adult volume by the age of three.

As recently as twenty years ago, it was thought that brain development stopped in early childhood. Neuroscientists have since discovered that further phases of major development take place until the age of about twelve, and then again in the teenage years. The adolescent brain undergoes extensive remodelling as teens refine their communication, learning and social skills. Some experts believe these changes help explain why teenagers can be so impulsive and difficult to handle: their brains aren't fully developed until they reach the age of twenty-five. (We'll be talking more about the teen brain in the next session.)

A number of pioneering researchers have sought to harness what they've learned about young brains to provide practical advice for parents helping children gradually learn to regulate their emotions and think more clearly. One of the leaders in this field is the American neuropsychiatrist Dr Daniel Siegel. In his book *The Whole-Brain Child*, co-authored with Dr Tina Payne Bryson, he provides a simplified portrait of the brain as being divided into two halves – a little like the floors of a two-storey house:

- **Downstairs brain.** This is the primitive part of the brain that controls all the things newborn babies can do – breathing, eating, sleeping, blinking and so on. The 'downstairs' brain is where our emotions happen. It also houses the amygdala – a tiny, almond-shaped component that serves as the brain's 'smoke alarm' – and is constantly scanning for danger.

● **Upstairs brain.** Think of a light-filled study lined with books. Also known as the 'prefrontal cortex', this part of the brain allows us to think clearly, plan for the future, make decisions, solve problems, use language and empathize with others. This part of the brain has a kind of 'neural wi-fi' that allows us to understand what others are feeling and respond appropriately. The prefrontal cortex is fully developed only when a child reaches early adulthood.

● **The stairway.** In adults, there is a kind of metaphorical 'stairway' linking the 'upstairs' brain and the 'downstairs' brain, with chemical messengers constantly relaying information between the floors. This 'stairway' allows us to exercise a degree of control over our emotions and think before we act. We are strengthening this connection every time we help our child to calm down or reflect on their behaviour and problem-solve.

Growing up is fundamentally about learning how to ensure all these parts of the brain work together in harmony. Even for adults, maintaining this balance is not always an easy task – as any parent who has ever regretted firing off an angry email to a teacher or shouting at their child in the supermarket can attest. For young children, regulating emotions is made many times harder by the fact that their 'upstairs' brains take years to develop fully. They are therefore much more vulnerable to being hijacked by big feelings arising in the 'downstairs' brain at any time – what Dr Siegel calls 'flipping your lid'.

The 'downstairs' brain is so powerful because it is in charge of the 'fight-or-flight' response that evolved to keep us alive. When our Neolithic ancestors encountered a rampaging woolly mammoth, the amygdala – the brain's 'smoke alarm' – would send a message to the body to start pumping out stress hormones such as cortisol and adrenaline in preparation for one of three things:

- **Flight.** We feel a rush of fear, and the body gears up to escape.

- **Fight.** We feel a flash of anger, and the body prepares to attack.

- **Freeze.** We are frozen to the spot in terror.

We may not face life-threatening situations very often these days, but our brain's fight-flight-or-freeze response can still be triggered many times each day. Our modern-day equivalents of woolly mammoths can be anything from our children squabbling to a stressful parents' evening or feeling judged by our mother-in-law. Think of the frisson of fear that runs through us when our child doesn't return home on time, or the surge of anger we experience at being cut up in traffic on the school run.

We may struggle to manage our own 'downstairs' brain – but a child's still-growing 'upstairs' brain finds it even more difficult to keep a flood of fear or anger in perspective. When the brain's 'smoke alarm' has been triggered, the 'stairway' that normally allows the 'upstairs' brain to control strong impulses is blocked. Messages can no longer pass between the two levels – it's as if a child's brain has filled up with smoke.

As any parent knows, there are different types of meltdowns. At times, a child may deliberately turn on the tears and screams as part of a calculated strategy by the 'upstairs' brain to try to get what they want. It's usually easy to tell such a performance from the real thing, but if you're in any doubt, take five deep breaths and ask your 'inner parent' for guidance. At other times, a child will be genuinely hijacked by their 'downstairs' brain and won't be able to control themselves. If the fight-or-flight response has been activated in this way, then your child's ability to listen to your attempts to reason with them through logical arguments goes out of the window.

Children who have found themselves 'flipping their lid' like this have often told me that they felt so overwhelmed and confused that they didn't know what they were doing. They had become so upset that they weren't able to grasp how much their behaviour had affected their parents. Some mums and dads find this surprising: how could they not remember the horrible things they said? Or the toy they threw at their sibling? But children may genuinely not know the answers to these questions. When they've been taken over by their 'downstairs' brain, the logical prefrontal cortex has gone offline. They can no longer think through the consequences of their actions clearly.

This loss of control can be accompanied by deep feelings of shame. Children realize they have let their parents down and can sense their disappointment. After they calm down, they may say the following sorts of things:

- 'I don't know why I hit him.'

- 'I don't remember lashing out.'

- 'I blacked out.'

- 'I can't control my temper.'

- 'I feel very sorry for what I did.'

- 'I feel ashamed of myself.'

- 'I feel bad for being naughty.'

From 'fight or flight' to 'tend and befriend'

The first thing to do when confronted with your child's meltdown is to check in with yourself. Notice the sensations in your body and the kinds of thoughts popping into your head. Take five deep breaths. Your ability to remain as centred as you can is the single greatest antidote to your child's distress, since they will take their emotional cue from you. Once you feel calmer, it will be easier to consult your 'inner parent' and consciously choose what to do to help your child cope with their strong feelings.

Of course, this is not always easy. One of the problems with tantrums is that they can so easily prove contagious. If we're not careful, we can find that our child's meltdown triggers our own 'smoke alarm' – especially if we're already having a bad day or feel that everything's going wrong. Before we know it, we're stuck in a shouting match with our screaming, tearful child. Afterwards, we may feel racked with guilt and question our own judgement, wondering why it was so hard for us to keep our cool.

We can be particularly vulnerable to this kind of contagion if a child's frustration and hostility triggers memories of dimly remembered events from our own childhood. We may be overtaken by a sense of hopelessness, injustice or unfairness that seems out of all proportion to the situation at hand. As we saw in Session 5, these unexpectedly strong feelings might be an echo of the despair we felt as children when our parents were shouting at us. Or we might experience an uncharacteristic wave of anger – perhaps a replay of the resentment we felt when we were scolded harshly by our own mum or dad. Even remnants of emotional pain from our past romantic relationships can be rekindled when we find ourselves in conflict with our children.

There is no need to analyse such feelings too deeply – it is enough to notice them, observe them and breathe through them, always trying to approach them with an attitude of curiosity rather than judgement. This is also a great time to remember to be kind to yourself. We can feel so shaken, shocked or bruised when our child has lashed out that it's important to do our best to take a moment to nurture ourselves before attempting to respond to their distress.

If your child is in the grip of a 'downstairs' brain tantrum, then it's no use trying to use logic and reason to explain to them that what they're doing is wrong, or to try to talk them out of feeling bad. With the 'stairway' between the 'upstairs' and 'downstairs' brain filled up with smoke, they won't be able to understand what you're saying.

There is no ready-made formula for helping any one child to calm down. What works will depend on the situation and your individual child. When you find yourself facing your child's meltdown, take a moment to pause and silently ask yourself:

- What do I need in this moment?

- What does my child need?

If you can be still for a moment, you may well find your 'inner parent' comes up with the answers.

Power of a hug

Holding your child close to you can be comforting as long as you are feeling calm and in control yourself. Even though a part of you may resist the idea of rewarding your child for their unacceptable behaviour, you will be better placed to soothe them if you can put your own hurt and frustration aside. You can deal with the fact that you didn't like the way they behaved later. Giving them a hug or holding them close to you can also release oxytocin, the bonding hormone, which promotes a feeling of well-being and reduces production of the stress hormone cortisol. As we saw in Session 1, a hug also stimulates the Vagus nerve, which helps bring their stress levels back into balance.

Of course, this 'tend-and-befriend' approach – to use the term coined by Dr Shelley Taylor – does not work for all children at all times: some won't like to be touched when they are in the midst of a meltdown, particularly older children or boys, though they might appreciate a hug afterwards. Your 'inner parent' will know when a hug is the best response.

Below are some more possibilities for responding to tantrums that other parents have found helpful.

Before the tantrum strikes

- **Know your child's triggers.** Identify the times or situations that make a tantrum most likely and try to minimize the build-up of stress where possible. Perhaps your child is more vulnerable after a long day at school, after playing on their Xbox, or when they're hungry, tired or excited. When you know from past experience what kinds of situations are likely to cause problems, you can be on the lookout for signs that things are escalating and try your best to calm your child down before they hit the point of no return.

- **Reflect feelings.** Before their emotions spiral out of control, it can help to validate a child's frustration by showing you are curious about how they might be feeling, without being pulled into their drama. Show you are trying to understand with statements like, 'I can see you are getting frustrated and annoyed right now,' or 'I know it's hard when I interrupt your computer game to ask you to come to the table.' It is, of course, important to be fair and firm and stick to your boundaries. Nevertheless, empathizing at this early stage helps a child feel heard and can defuse a build-up of resentment before it gets out of hand.

- **Share your own feelings.** When appropriate, share your own feelings with your child – helping them to learn that they are not the only person whose well-being matters. For example, 'I'm getting really irritated and annoyed right now. I need some time out to relax before I lose my temper.' Providing your child with information about your feelings in a non-accusatory tone is a great way to model how to deal with difficult emotions and see life from another's point of view.

- **Burn off excess energy.** Children need plenty of opportunities to use up their abundant energy – but many kids are sat at classroom desks all day. Children are often calmer after a good run around or a few minutes of dancing, rough-and-tumble play or sports. Maybe they need some cushions or beanbags to roll around on, a go on a trampoline or to play outside in the fresh air. There is a growing body of research reinforcing what our parents' generation is fond of telling us: children tend to be more well-balanced and healthier if they are given regular opportunities to immerse themselves in nature. Even if you live in a built-up area, making time to explore a park or tear across a green can make a big difference.

In the heat of the moment

- **See through your child's eyes.** Remind yourself that your child's distress is genuine, even if their problem appears insignificant. Although they may seem to be over-reacting to a trivial issue, their frustration is very real.

- **Speak softly.** When your child is having a tantrum, your ability to provide a calm presence is more powerful than anything you can say. It can work well to speak in low, soothing and comforting tones.

- **Get down to their level.** For younger children, it might be helpful to sit or crouch down next to them, all the while speaking gently.

- **Distraction.** Distracting a child can be very effective as it activates the seeking part of the 'downstairs' brain. Engaging their curiosity in this way can release dopamine, a feel-good chemical that reduces stress and helps them feel interested and motivated.

- **Breathe the anger.** Imagine with your child that a fire has gone off in their brain and you are going to help them blow all those flames away.

- **Take a break.** With an older child, you could say something like, 'We are both starting to get angry here. Shall we both take time out to calm down, then talk about this later when we can come up with a better solution?' State clearly that this is for a set time – say fifteen minutes – to ensure your child knows you are not abandoning them or running away from the problem. Returning to resolve the dispute after the break shows your child that you can work things out together, and models the kind of conflict-resolution skills that will serve them well as adults.

In the aftermath

- **Post-tantrum analysis.** When your child has calmed down, take the opportunity to engage their 'upstairs' brain to think through what has just happened, what they could have done differently and what they have learned. You can also take a moment to ask yourself if you might approach a similar situation differently in the future.

- **Mindful listening.** When you run through what happened with your child, listen to their side of the story and resist the temptation to interrupt and argue if you do not agree. Allow them to share their perspective.

- **Validate.** Give your child permission to feel angry and explain that anger is a normal, healthy emotion. For example, 'I would feel angry too, if that had happened to me. I can understand why you got angry – it sounded like it felt really unfair for you, but screaming and hitting your sister is not the right way to deal with it.' Understanding is not the same as excusing disrespectful behaviour: ask your 'inner parent' whether it would be appropriate to introduce consequences for something your child has done and explain to them clearly why you are doing so. Children need to learn that lashing out, swearing or hitting people is not okay – and that anger can be channelled in more positive ways, such as by burning off energy through exercise or play.

- **Learn and grow.** Take each meltdown as an opportunity to help strengthen connections in your child's 'upstairs' brain, rather than slipping into cycles of blame and shame. Ask them what was going on for them and give them space to respond. Every time that your child gets angry is an opportunity for you both to learn how you could approach a similar situation differently next time. Draw a distinction between your child and their behaviour. We can say that we regret what happened but we still love them.

- **Forgiveness.** Perhaps the best thing you can do for yourself and your child is to forgive yourself when you inevitably do lose your temper or find it difficult to remain calm. These are not easy situations to manage – and it's important to give yourself credit for doing the best you can.

What to avoid

- **Time out.** It's fine to give a child space to calm down, but isolating them as a punishment can cause them to internalize feelings of shame and abandonment, and question whether they are loved. Putting a child in 'time out' can also deprive them of a valuable opportunity to learn how to manage their feelings with an adult they trust by their side. There's also a danger that the original cause of your child's upset will be left unresolved, unless you are able to have a conversation when you've both calmed down.

- **Taking it personally.** It's natural to feel upset, but it's important to try not to take your child's behaviour personally or to interpret it as a reflection of your parenting skills. This takes a great deal of self-compassion, but the kinder you are to yourself the better. Raising children is not easy – and tantrums are part of the journey.

Carly: 'He doesn't seem to hear me'

'When Leo's in a meltdown I keep asking, "What's wrong? What's the matter?" But he doesn't seem to hear me. I get extremely frustrated and often think it's my fault. I feel a real sense of failure for not being able to keep my child under control. Then I end up losing my temper with him and before I know it we're both screaming at each other. I hate to

Continued . . .

admit it, but at times like this I feel a real hostility towards my own child. When he's calmed down, I ask him again what was the matter and he says he doesn't know. I feel like I'm pressurizing him because he genuinely can't come up with an answer. I can tell he feels like he's let me down, and that makes me feel even worse.'

When Carly gains a greater understanding of the way Leo's 'upstairs' brain has gone blank during his meltdown, she sees that reasoning with him won't work. Even more importantly, she sees that it's vital to manage her own reaction – so she doesn't go into fight-or-flight mode as well. Carly realizes Leo's outbursts are not a sign of failure on either side: if anything they are proof that the fight-or-flight mechanism that has kept our species alive is in full working order. We can't teach a child much when their 'downstairs' brain has taken over. But by working through what happened afterwards, Carly can help Leo develop the crucial 'upstairs' brain skills that will help him gradually to learn how to manage his emotions more successfully.

The next time Leo begins to lose it, Carly takes five deep breaths and watches her own response to his screams and sobs: a feeling that she's tensing up all over and getting hot. By remaining mindful in this way, she has a better chance of staying calm even as Leo is consumed by anger. Carly notices that when she doesn't allow her own reaction to spiral out of control, Leo's behaviour doesn't seem quite as distressing. She's no longer gripped by feelings of failure – and sometimes Leo seems to calm down quicker than he did in the past.

'I'm definitely not perfect – I still sometimes lose my temper when Leo's screaming. I can still get in a real mood with him. But I've hung a picture of a heart up on the kitchen wall: it's a symbol of how much I love Leo despite everything. Whenever I start to feel myself getting angry, seeing the heart reminds me to take a moment to step back and remember that it's not going to help me or Leo if I'm unable to show him how to stay calm.'

Further possibilities

Here are some strategies that other parents have used to help their children gradually learn better management of their feelings over time:

- **Meltdown diary.** Make a note in the journal on page 259 of when tantrums occur to see if there are any patterns that reveal triggers which can then be minimized. The key questions are:

  - What caused the tantrum?
  - Can you identify specific factors such as being hungry, tired or hot, or feeling overwhelmed by something that happened at school?
  - What kind of behaviour did your child display?
  - What were the consequences of the behaviour?

One mum realized that her child's rages tended to erupt when *she* was feeling most stressed – particularly at the end of a workday. Seeing clearly that the meltdowns were linked to her own moods helped this mum give herself permission to take more frequent breaks. By showing herself greater kindness in this way, she was able to remain calmer – benefiting both herself and her son.

- **Anger thermometer.** Get some pens, paper and coloured card and work with your child to make a picture of an 'anger thermometer' with a gauge going from 0 (calm) to 10 (when their anger has exploded like a volcano). You can use this as a tool to connect with your child by exploring how their anger works. Begin by discussing what triggers your child's anger – maintaining an attitude of non-judgement and curiosity. Typical triggers might include:

  - Tiredness
  - Hunger
  - Being told to do something that they don't want to do
  - A particular time of day
  - A hard day at school/exam stress
  - Difficulties with friendships or a particular teacher

- Stress over homework
- Spending too long playing on screens
- Fighting with siblings

Then discuss how their anger builds up by talking through specific examples of when they lost their temper. Ask them to identify the warning signs in terms of physical sensations in their body and assign a number from the anger thermometer to reflect the intensity of the feeling that goes with it. These are some of the common signs children have described to me, but there are many others:

- Foot starts tapping
- Fidgeting
- Feeling hot
- Breathing fast and shallow
- Muscles tense and jaw clenches

Next, ask your child about the kinds of thoughts that make them angry. Perhaps they feel they have been treated unfairly, a brother or sister is annoying them, or they don't want to be told what to do by adults.

It's helpful to ask them to chart their 'point of no return' – the number on the thermometer where they have become so angry that it is impossible for them to calm down and they need to be left alone for a few minutes before they can begin to settle.

Next time anger builds, encourage your child to describe the intensity of their feeling by saying a number from the thermometer. This will help them to catch themselves and interrupt the cycle.

This exercise is even more powerful if you work through your own anger thermometer in parallel. This helps to normalize anger and creates a space for you both to support each other to manage your moods. For example, if you're feeling under strain you can tell your child, 'I'm on a five now', and they will be able to understand clearly what's going on for you.

Talking through thoughts and feelings in this way helps your child to engage their 'upstairs' brain and start to become more self-aware. With your help, they can recognize their warning signs earlier and increasingly learn to manage their feelings. Rather than being a source of shame, each new meltdown is another opportunity to learn more about how their anger works. (The 'thermometer' approach can also be used with other intense emotions, such as anxiety or fear, which we explore in more depth in Session 8.)

● **Glitter jar.** The psychologist Dr Christopher Willard recommends a novel exercise: work with children to make a 'glitter jar' out of a plastic water bottle or jar. Choose three differently coloured glitters – one for thoughts, one for feelings and one for impulses to act on feelings (and maybe add some food colouring for fun). Shake the jar and show the children how confused the pattern becomes. Ask them to imagine what kind of events could cause the equivalent chaos in their minds. Being late for school? An argument with a sibling? Being told off by a teacher? Then show them what happens as they remain quiet and still: their thoughts, feelings and impulses gradually settle. The idea is to demonstrate the advantage of pausing before you act.

● **Visual cues.** In some schools, teachers agree to give certain children special cards that they can show the teacher when they are feeling overwhelmed and need a moment of quiet. Some parents use the cards at home with children to help them manage their anger. You could also agree that your child will use a special hand signal – such as a raised palm – if they're struggling to cope or sense a meltdown building.

● **A quiet den.** If you have enough space, create a special place with blankets, cushions or a favourite cuddly toy where a child can retreat if they need to calm down. This need not take up too much room: one mum allowed her young daughter to go and sit in a wardrobe, which they had agreed she would use when she needed a moment to cool down.

- **Label.** Working with younger children to label their feelings helps them to learn to handle their emotions better. This is best done when they have calmed down enough to engage their 'upstairs' brain. For example, if your child has just had a meltdown, you could ask them what words would best describe how they felt, such as 'angry', 'sad' or 'frustrated'. The act of naming feelings in this way helps children to learn to handle them when they occur in the future. You can also use visual cues to help your child describe what they were experiencing: pictures, books, 'feeling flashcards' or a 'feelings jar'. (For further reading, see Resources, page 244.)

- **Name or draw anger.** Younger children in particular may find it helpful to draw their anger or give it a name. Expressing their feelings by drawing brightly coloured scribbles, blobs and splotches can be a healthy, creative way to let off steam. Some children may also enjoy drawing their anger as a scary monster or a villain from a favourite story or film.

'Worry Monsters' and 'Bully Planets'

Drawing worries as figures such as a fairytale 'Worry Monster' or cartoon character can help children to put some distance between themselves and their concerns, and enable them to see worrying as a habit they have acquired, not an integral part of who they are.

For example, when I asked ten-year-old Ella to try to come up with a name for her stream of negative thoughts, she spontaneously said, 'Bully Planet' – visualizing a sinister-looking celestial object beaming self-critical thoughts into her mind. Though this might sound like a disturbing image, it was immensely liberating for Ella to start to think about her worries in this new way. Whenever Ella started to worry, she was able to tell herself, *'Bully Planet's taking over again,'* which immediately put some distance between herself and her worrisome thoughts. Or, when Ella was too upset to remember to say this, her mother asked her, *'Is Bully Planet saying nasty things again?'*

Eventually, Ella was able to enter into a dialogue with Bully Planet, saying, *'I'm not listening to you! Stop trying to make me feel bad! I don't believe everything you say!'* In one session, she wrote down what Bully Planet was saying then screwed up the paper and threw it into a rubbish bin. Of course, such an exercise is not a permanent 'cure' for worrying – but it helped Ella to feel that she was more in control of her negative thoughts and feelings.

Sensitive children

Over the years, I have come across many parents who say there is something 'different' about their child. Their son or daughter seems to be particularly sensitive and to feel things more deeply than other children. They can be acutely sensitive to sensory overload – especially loud noise or variations in temperature. They may burst into tears or throw tantrums easily, but also seem to think very deeply and have huge hearts. They might be particularly disturbed by news stories about global problems, suffering or injustice and seem burdened beyond their years. Though they may be highly intelligent, they may struggle to cope with the noise and bustle of a mainstream school and say they don't feel listened to or understood.

Teachers or mental health professionals often struggle to know how to categorize such children, who don't seem to fit an official diagnostic box such as autism or ADHD (see box, page 158). I've worked with many parents who know their children are not suffering from some sort of disorder, but they do seem to require more understanding and nurturing than their peers, or even their siblings.

Dr Elaine Aron, an American psychologist, uses the phrase 'Highly Sensitive Person' (HSP) to describe such children, whom she estimates make up about 20 per cent of the US population. Though this is not a term commonly used in Britain, I have come across many such children, whom I have observed display a number of the following characteristics:

- Feels emotions more intensely than other children

- Highly sensitive to noise, taste, heat or other forms of sensory overload

- Takes things personally

- Very loving and wants to connect physically and emotionally

- Deep thinker who can get lost in their own world

- Has intense meltdowns

- Takes criticism to heart – and holds on to it for days

- Frequent worrying and anxiety

- Dislikes change

- Can burst into tears or lose their temper easily

- Highly empathic to other children's feelings

- Strong sense of fairness and justice

- Intense negative reactions to lying in any form

- Strong affinity with animals or passion for environmental issues

- Easily drained but may have difficulty sleeping

- Questions rules that don't make sense

- Highly attuned to what adults around them may be feeling

- Unusually sensitive to textures of clothing

Our society isn't geared to people with such sensitive temperaments, and these children don't tend to fit in easily to our existing schools. Because they tend to take things so personally, they can feel crushed by the kind of telling off or punishment that other children would take in their stride. As parents, we can see that such setbacks have a much greater impact on their self-esteem, and they may be especially prone to internalizing a negative view of themselves.

While we are naturally concerned about the emotional difficulties these sensitive children experience, we need to recognize the enormous potential their sensitivity, compassion and empathy hold for themselves, their families and the wider community. As a culture, we tend to see this kind of sensitivity as a weakness – even though these children's empathy for their fellow humans, animals and the environment might be precisely the qualities the world needs right now.

The American professors Thomas Boyce and Bruce Ellis argue that sensitive children can be viewed as 'orchids'. Like these beautiful, delicate flowers, these children are acutely sensitive to their environment. They can flower into unusually talented and creative adults if nurtured properly, but they can easily wither if they don't receive the right care. Most children, however, resemble 'dandelions' – they are far more resilient and can thrive in a wide range of environments. Boyce and Ellis are investigating whether genetic factors may play a role in whether a child is an 'orchid' or a 'dandelion', and how we can help all types of children to thrive.

There are no hard-and-fast rules for how to raise an 'orchid' child. What we can do, however, is to explore our own attitudes towards their sensitivity. Do we see it as a defect? Or can we embrace the unique contribution these children can make when they are accepted and understood? It's easy to get caught up in what seems to be 'wrong' with our child – but the more we can see them with fresh eyes and keep an open mind, the more we will come to appreciate the quirks and strengths that this degree of sensitivity brings. Even if others can't always see your child's gifts, trust your instincts. Your 'inner parent' knows the kind of nurturing and understanding your child needs. Though this is a new field, there are some great books on sensitive children and I have listed several on page 236 of the References section.

When a Child Is Diagnosed with ADHD

Growing numbers of children and teenagers are being diagnosed with Attention Deficit Hyperactivity Disorder (ADHD) or other neurodevelopmental disorders. Such a child will have significant difficulties in the following areas, in at least two environments (e.g. at home and at school), compared to another child of the same age and ability:

● **Hyperactivity.** Constantly fidgety, has difficulty sitting still, runs around a lot and is often restless at night.

● **Concentration.** Finds it very hard to focus on a task, follow instructions or complete things.

● **Impulsivity.** Acts without thinking through consequences, blurts things out, talks excessively and struggles to wait their turn.

(In some cases, where hyperactivity is not a problem, a child showing these symptoms may be diagnosed with Attention Deficit Disorder (ADD)).

Every child experiences their symptoms in different ways, but I find that parents whose child has ADHD tend to encounter a number of similar issues. Schools and individual teachers vary widely in the degree to which they understand these kinds of conditions, or even acknowledge that they exist. Some show the patience and care that can make all the difference, but others are less sympathetic – and may even assume ADHD is some sort of myth, or an excuse for bad behaviour. A child can end up being scapegoated and find themselves stuck with a label of the 'naughty one', the 'class clown' or the 'troublemaker'.

For parents, it's easy to slip into a sense of failure or to assume you're doing something wrong when your child proves difficult to manage. It can be hard to see their strengths when they are viewed as a 'problem' by their school, and painful when the system isn't geared up to provide the nurturing environment they need. In our fatigue and frustration, we can easily lose sight of the positives – and particularly the enormous energy and enthusiasm that children with ADHD can channel into their passions. It's no coincidence that there are many highly successful athletes, film stars, musicians and top executives in the business world who have this diagnosis.

As with any parenting challenge, the first task is to find your own calm centre before making any decisions. There are a lot of misunderstandings around ADHD and it's important to seek specialist advice and avoid any temptation to go online and diagnose your child yourself. Obtaining a professional diagnosis is essential to navigating the system and accessing the right help – a little like having a passport to visit a foreign country. But a label is still only a set of words: every child's experience is unique. It's important not to confuse your child with their diagnosis.

Children don't like to be 'different' and the risk of attaching too much significance to a label like ADHD is that they may internalize a sense that there's something wrong with them. As with any medical diagnosis, these sorts of labels can form a screen that makes it harder to see a child clearly. It's not wrong to apply such labels, but they shouldn't obscure the unique qualities each child possesses.

We all need to feel accepted, acknowledged and understood, and the most important thing is to create a space of awareness where you approach your child with an attitude of curiosity – and look beyond their symptoms to see the individual beneath.

*

The five key points
Managing meltdowns

- Anger is contagious: check in with yourself when faced with your child's tantrum.

- Screaming and tears may be a sign the 'downstairs' brain has taken over.

- Pause and ask, 'What do I need? What does my child need?'

- You can't use logic and reason with your child until they've calmed down.

- Use each meltdown as a learning opportunity for you and your child.

Session 8

Surviving the teenage years

When it comes to raising teenagers, here are some of the comments I often hear from parents:

- 'I'm dreading the teenage years – and my son's only eight.'

- 'There's so much pressure these days. I don't know how I would have coped as a teen in today's world.'

- 'I'm just crossing my fingers and hoping we get through.'

- 'I remember what it was like – I couldn't wait to grow up.'

- 'There he goes again – a typical teenager.'

These days, it's not unusual to hear parents expressing their fears about what the roller-coaster teenage years may bring when their children are barely out of their pushchairs. Almost everyone feels that the pressures their sons and daughters are facing are somehow much greater than those they remember from their own adolescence, and they worry if they are doing the right things. Of course, it's impossible to know for sure whether the teenage years really *are* more difficult today, but there's certainly a widespread feeling that the final stages of the transition to adulthood have somehow grown more challenging and intense than ever.

Mums and dads contrast their childhood memories of endless hours' running around the park unsupervised and climbing trees with their own children's packed schedules and ever-increasing homework. They worry about the impact of screens on developing brains, or whether their teenagers will cope with the pressures of social media – new phenomena that weren't around when we were growing up. Parents can feel particularly anxious to ensure that their children get to their first-choice school – and even if they do, they may wonder if it's the right environment for them. We're living in a society where the gap between haves and have-nots has widened in recent years, and many parents feel immense pressure, and go to extraordinary lengths, to give their child every imaginable chance of success.

It's perhaps no coincidence that there is so much demand for professional support for teenagers facing emotional difficulties. Exam stress is one of the most common problems I see, driven by the growing pressure on students to perform from a young age and fears of what may happen if they don't get the right grades. Of course, some ups and downs are inevitable – all teenagers experience a degree of self-consciousness and the natural growing pains of finding out who they are. But more and more suffer from crippling anxiety attacks, low self-esteem, chronic problems with concentration, eating disorders, worries over body image or self-harm. Whatever they may be going through, all teenagers have one thing in common: they hate to be stereotyped and crave the recognition as individuals that they deserve.

While it's important to talk about the problems, it's equally important to remember to celebrate the gifts the teenage years can bring. This is a unique phase of potential – bursting with just the kind of energy, creativity and idealism that we need to build a brighter future. But there's no question that channelling these energies in a positive direction can at times be very hard – for parents as well as for teenagers.

It can seem impossible to know what's going on in your teenager's mind, and they often don't seem to know either. One moment they can be chatting and laughing, only to withdraw or snap at you the next, their reactions flaring up in response to minor setbacks, or an innocent request to help with the chores or tidy their room.

It's natural to think wistfully of the days when your little one was all smiley and cute, and start wondering who is this person living under your roof, who barely leaves their room, communicates largely in grunts, eye-rolls and door-slamming, and is constantly forgetting things. Even though we may expect frosty silences, mood swings and arguments as a normal part of the teenage experience, it can be tough to discover that the times they need us the most are the very times they are most likely to push us away.

It's much easier to organize a child's life when they're younger, but trying to control a teenager never works. As parents, you naturally want them to develop a healthy sense of autonomy and independence – but it can be hard to strike a balance between intervening to protect them and allowing them to learn from their mistakes. Teens may complain, argue and resist the boundaries you set, but, just like younger children, they need limits in order to feel safe. The stakes can feel so much higher than they did a few years earlier because teenagers are more prone to taking risks or succumbing to peer pressure. At the same time, questions over further education and jobs are coming into sharper focus, creating another layer of uncertainty.

Teenage moods can prove contagious and it's easy for us to become entangled in their drama. We may see with our logical mind that we are over-reacting, but it may only be when we look more deeply at what is going on that we realize they are reawakening long-buried hurts dating back to our own adolescence. We may even be surprised to find ourselves feeling a pang of envy when confronted with our teenagers' enthusiasm and idealism. However much of a handful they may be, we can't deny that they have their whole lives ahead of them. We can choose to meet such feelings with compassion – and ask whether they may be a signal for us to rediscover some of their youthful qualities in our own lives.

There is no simple solution to any of these challenges. But one thing is for sure: any parent confronted with a difficult teenager will be in a far better position to maintain a HEART-centred connection if they can find their own calm centre. Mindfulness can help us notice when we're being pulled into an unthinking reaction that will make it much harder to tune in to the guidance of our 'inner parent' and provide the kind of quietly confident leadership a teenager needs. In this session, we look in more depth at some of the common problems facing teenagers today and explore ways to strengthen our connection – even in the toughest of times.

Beth: 'I feel shocked and helpless'

When Beth's fifteen-year-old daughter Emily first came to see me, she walked into the room with downcast eyes and hunched shoulders, and hid her face behind her hair. She barely spoke, but when she did, she tugged the sleeve of her sweater over her hands. Beth's concerns reflected many of the issues I often see in my practice:

'I'm worried because Emily's coming up to her GCSE year. She's in the top sets for Maths and English, but she lacks confidence. She won't go out without make-up because she thinks everyone's staring at her – it's got so bad I'm actually seriously thinking about getting her to get her eyebrows and eyelashes dyed so we can actually get out of the house on time.

'And this is the bit that really shocks me. I've discovered she's been self-harming. I was stunned. I'd never heard of this before. How could anybody want to cut themselves with a razor? Let alone my daughter – she was such a sweet little girl at primary school. Whenever she disappears into her bedroom, I'm really worried that she might do it again. I feel I've maybe gone to an extreme, but I've locked everything

sharp away. I don't know if that's really the right thing to do, if I'm making the right choices here. I just want her to go to school and build some confidence. It destroys me that she's hurting herself.

'My husband says that I've always been over-protective and that Emily's too dependent on me. He's probably right, but the minute I back off she has a meltdown and what mum stands back and lets her daughter fall apart? Even simple things end up being a problem. For example, I'd like her to go down to the shop and get me a few things, but she won't even go into our local Tesco's because she thinks everyone's looking at her. Even if I go with her she thinks she'll see girls from her school and they'll start posting nasty comments about her on Facebook.

'It's so different to when I was younger. I was bullied, but at least then you only had to deal with it during school time. Now it continues out of hours, and it's into the weekend as well. I really feel for Emily, my heart goes out to her. I don't think I could have coped with that when I was younger.

'I feel like a bad mum, and that I've somehow caused all this. It's all very well reading the advice, but the fact is that it's hard to stop beating yourself up and blaming yourself when things go wrong with your child. I bought a meditation CD, hoping that it would help to calm my nerves, but it just made me feel like more of a failure, because I couldn't empty my mind and stop thinking about my daughter. Emily's always texting me when I'm at work or I'm in meetings. How do you manage that? She needs to stop needing my reassurance so much. She's too dependent on me, she's just a mess, and to be honest I am too. All I want is for Emily to be happy.'

*

Wired for risk

It used to be commonplace to blame teenagers' mood swings or irritability on their 'hormones'. But neuroscientists have learned more in recent years about how the adolescent brain undergoes a very distinct phase of development. As Adriana Galván, an associate professor at the University of California, puts it: from the point of view of brain science, teenagers are neither 'overgrown children' nor 'mini-adults'. Though neuroscience is still a very young discipline, it does seem that something quite unique is going on inside teenagers' skulls that influences the way they think, feel and behave.

As we saw in Session 7, the brain rapidly forms new neural pathways until the age of about twelve, when it starts removing connections it no longer needs, like a gardener snipping at a rosebush. This 'neural pruning' continues throughout the teenage years. The remaining connections are made faster through a process known as 'myelination', in which neurons are insulated with a sheath of fatty material. Because the brain develops from the back to the front, this upgrading process does not reach the prefrontal cortex – the 'upstairs' brain responsible for rational decision-making and self-control – until the twenties. Neuroscientists believe that evolving teenage brains are therefore simply incapable of exercising the same degree of judgement and self-control as adults – which won't be news to anybody with a teen living under their roof.

The way their brains develop seems to have a number of implications for the way teenagers behave:

● **Disregard for consequences.** Dr Daniel Siegel argues that teens are good at examining facts, but they can't always see the big picture of what might happen if they take a certain course of action. Though they may be fully aware of risks, they place more weight on the exciting potential benefits of taking a chance than what might happen if it all goes wrong. The limbic system in a teenage brain – which helps govern emotion – seems to derive more pleasure from risk-taking than an adult's does. With the logical prefrontal cortex still not fully developed, this may help explain why teenagers can be so impulsive.

• **Sensitivity to peer pressure.** According to the neuroscientist Professor Sarah-Jayne Blakemore, teenagers may be so acutely sensitive to their peers' opinions partly because their brains register the impact of being ostracized more acutely than adult brains. This helps explain why a teenage boy can easily succumb to pressure to smoke marijuana despite being fully aware of the risks, or why a teenage girl may give in to demands to send a naked selfie, even when she knows what could happen if the picture is shared. The desire to belong far outweighs fear of potential consequences.

• **Difficulty in seeing another's perspective.** The ability to 'mentalize' – or see a situation from another person's point of view – is still developing in teens. Neuroscientists have seen different patterns of brain activity in the teen brain compared to an adult brain during tasks that require thinking of others. One possible explanation is that teens use completely different strategies in social decision-making than adults. This might help explain why so many parents feel so exasperated with teenagers who seem incapable of seeing things from their point of view.

• **Interpretation of facial expressions.** Research by Dr Yolanda van Beek and Dr Judith Semon Dubas has provided intriguing evidence that teenagers may interpret facial expressions differently to adults. Their neuro-imaging experiment revealed that teens who were shown a picture of a neutral face experienced activation of their amygdala – the brain's 'smoke alarm' – creating a strongly negative reaction. In adults, the same photograph activated only the prefrontal cortex – the rational part of the 'upstairs' brain. Similarly, research by Dr Deborah Yurgelun-Todd suggested that teenagers have difficulty reading the faces of the adults around them. These findings could help explain why teens can be so hypersensitive and why they misinterpret neutral expressions from parents or teachers as signs of hostility.

Of course, it wouldn't make sense to reduce the accumulated research of the world's top neuroscientists into an excuse for reckless teenage behaviour. But it may make this behaviour easier to explain. In many respects, it is up to parents to play the role of a teenager's 'upstairs' brain on their behalf, coaching them to think through consequences or resist peer pressure to take dangerous risks. These kinds of conversations will not only help keep your teen out of trouble, but will also boost their brain by reinforcing neural connections associated with discernment and self-control.

Out of sync

In my work with teenagers, I've often been struck by the sheer numbers who seemed barely able to keep awake during our sessions. It was only relatively recently that I realized this wasn't a commentary on my failure to share their enthusiasm for the latest YouTube vlogger or bluff my way through Pokémon Go. When I asked them about their goals for our work together, they would often reply – yawning – 'To help me sleep.' Teenagers' traditional reluctance to drag themselves out of bed has tended to be treated as evidence of laziness. But researchers are starting to understand that there may be very real biological reasons why so many teens struggle to get up in the morning.

At about the age of ten to twelve, the release of melatonin – the hormone that aids sleep – shifts forward by roughly two hours, making it more difficult for teenagers to go to sleep and get up early. According to sleep researchers at the University of Oxford, asking a teen to get up at 7 a.m. to start school at 9 a.m. is a little like asking a fifty-five-year-old to get up at 5 a.m. No wonder, then, that so many teenagers feel sleepy well into mid-morning and seem to need such long lie-ins at weekends.

Though there's a strong biological case for teens starting lessons later, schools don't look likely to change their timetables any time soon. One way to reduce teenage sleep deficits might be to try to limit evening use of tablets or phones, which emit a low-level light in the blue wavelength that alerts the biological clock and may make it harder to sleep. Studies have also shown that using technology such as e-readers in the hour prior to sleep can delay the release of melatonin. Helping teenagers to learn about the importance of getting into a good sleep routine may help them to mitigate the worst effects of lost shut-eye.

Connecting with your teen

In an ideal world, we'd never feel short of time to spend with our teenagers. In reality, carving out even a few minutes to make a connection can seem impossible. Teenagers tend to be far more interested in spending time with their friends or retreating into their bedrooms to WhatsApp or text than hanging out with their parents. It can be a real challenge to find ways to spend time together, even though we know how important it is to keep our HEART-centred connection strong during these formative years.

Choose your moment

In our urge to connect, it's natural to start asking your teenager questions as soon as they walk through the front door. It's always worth pausing to ask your 'inner parent' whether your teen may need a bit of time to decompress. There may be easier opportunities to catch up without putting them on the spot – such as while driving or watching a bit of early-evening television. Many teens seem to want to offload late at night after finishing their revision, so your best chance for a chat may be round the kitchen table at midnight, or at the end of their bed. Even if you're struggling to connect on a daily basis, don't underestimate the power of sitting down for a family meal once a week, even if your teens grumble. Or call a 'family meeting', where everyone has an opportunity to share their point of view while everyone else listens. This can be a very effective way to ensure that the whole family – including your teen – feels respected and heard. You may want to consider making such occasions a phone-free zone – for adults and children.

Freedom versus independence

As your teens get older, there's no easy way to strike a balance between the need to give them more independence and the necessity to set boundaries that feel right for you while they're still living in your home. Of course you want to protect your teenager, but on the other hand no teen will benefit from being micro-managed or feeling that you don't trust them. Take it one step at a time. See how they respond to a certain degree of increased responsibility and let them show you how they get on. Ask your 'inner parent': are they ready to handle a little bit more freedom, or have you given them more than they can currently cope with? They will only be able to prove they are competent if you set your expectations on the high side – and they have to be allowed to make a few mistakes along the way.

Have confidence and be honest with yourself about how you feel: you don't have to give in to every demand. Try your best not to over-react or take it too personally if they push your boundaries and get angry with you for not giving them what they want. Teenagers will naturally want more freedom and push limits, but if they break a clear agreement then you may feel it's appropriate to introduce consequences.

Finding ways to spend time with a teenager who's more interested in going to parties or hanging out with groups of friends can be a challenge, but it's important to invest the extra effort: you need to remain their primary emotional support, rather than outsourcing this role to their peers. Other teens can be a great source of camaraderie, but they simply don't have the wisdom, maturity or life experience to provide the guidance your teen will need in every situation. The bond you forge during the teenage years will form the foundation for your relationship as they grow into adulthood, so it's worth persevering as far as you can.

One way of bridging the gap is to welcome their friends into your home, whether it be for a meal, a barbecue or just dropping by at weekends or evenings. This doesn't mean you need to be a 'cool' mum or dad who tries to be one of the gang – teenagers still want parents to be parents. It's more about showing that you respect your teen and are interested in their friends. You obviously can't force your teenager to spend one-on-one time with you, but you can ask them about what they might enjoy doing with you from time to time. Then intentionally carve out a specific time for a shared activity, whether it's an outing such as going to the cinema or on a shopping trip, or just sitting down and watching a box set. It's normal for teenagers to yo-yo in their connection with parents: sometimes close, sometimes drifting away. You can signal that the door is always open.

Words matter

It's also worth paying attention to the way you respond to your teenager's troubles. If your teenager begins pouring their heart out, it's tempting to draw on your own experience and say things like, 'I remember what it was like being a teenager – I was one too.' While we are doing our best to understand their perspective, the risk with using these kinds of phrases is that we can inadvertently sound as if we're not really listening. It's a little like the deflation we can feel after confiding in a friend and hearing them say, 'I know how you feel.' Part of us is silently insisting, 'No you don't!' It's the same for teenagers. We all need to feel heard.

As discussed in Session 5, when we feel under pressure we're more likely to slip into the kind of parenting styles we may have inherited from our own parents. We may catch ourselves using phrases we remember from our childhood, or thinking thoughts along these kinds of lines:

- 'She's the child, I'm the adult and she should just do what I say.'

- 'My parents used to shout at me and I turned out okay.'

- 'It's so hard being a parent, I can barely cope.'

- 'All he seems to want to do is play on his computer.'

- 'When I was young I was always out with my friends.'

- Any sentence starting with the phrase, 'Kids nowadays . . .' or 'Typical teenager . . .' should be avoided unless you want an eye-roll in response.

As far as you can, pause before you respond. Take five deep breaths and maintain awareness of your body. Keep some of your attention focused within. However challenging your teen's behaviour may be, the key is to model the kind of qualities you'd like to see them display – even if they may test you mightily in the process. Try to suspend judgement. I am often struck by how much teenagers fear disappointing their parents, however nonchalant they may appear. Deep down, many are concerned by the amount of distress and worry they may be causing and will often readily respond if you choose to extend an olive branch.

Setting aside your mask

Children tend to be highly perceptive, but teens have a laser-like ability to see through a lack of authenticity in any form. No matter what you say, they will notice how you are *being* – with other people, and in your relationship with your partner. They will be acutely aware of how much compassion you show to others, and particularly to yourself. It may not always seem like it, but they can also sense very clearly when adults like, respect and trust them – and are able to see them as a unique individual, regardless of how they may be behaving in that moment. Above all, in caring for your teen, try to remember to be kind to yourself. There will inevitably be times when you react to challenges in ways you might later regret. That's okay, and part of what it means to be a parent. Each moment is a new moment, and each day an opportunity to start again.

HEART-centred problem-solving

When a teenager comes to us with a problem, it's natural for us to want to come up with a solution. We may become very practical and engage the logical, solution-focused part of our minds. But there's something very powerful about remembering the Humility aspect of a HEART-centred connection. We are allowed to say, 'Do you know what? I don't understand what you're going through. Tell me more so I can learn.' Teenagers will often respond to this kind of honesty with far greater openness than if you find yourself playing the role of problem-solver. Of course we want to help them with their difficulties. But it can also be immensely powerful to share your vulnerability. This takes great courage, but teenagers will respect you for being able to say, 'I don't know.'

When problems do arise, it may help to explore the potential for adopting a joint approach – working with your teenager to find a way forward. We may remember our own parents being quite strict in the way they imposed boundaries, but we can all recognize that nobody likes to be lectured. There may be times when you do need to take firm action, particularly when a teenager's safety is at stake. But the advantage of working together on an issue where possible is that it gives a teenager the feeling that their views matter. The conversation starts with both of you on an equal footing: it's not about you knowing more or having more power.

The obvious danger with trying to lay down the law too forcefully is that it can backfire: an increasingly sneaky teenager will find new ways to break the rules without you even knowing. I often begin my therapy sessions with the simple observation that 'two heads are better than one'. I'm on a journey with the parents I work with – and they are the experts on themselves. My job is to help mums and dads find their own answers. Parents can do the same for their teens.

Teenage triggers

The teenage years can be so intense that it's not always easy – and often impossible – to provide the kind of assured leadership we might wish. We were all teenagers once, and it's inevitable that witnessing our own children going through these tumultuous times can reawaken some of the memories or feelings we'd prefer to forget. I've worked with many mums and dads who found that hearing about their child's struggles brought up images, feelings or physical sensations related to memories of what they had assumed was in their distant past. For example:

- 'My daughter being bullied triggers a painful memory of being victimized in the playground.'

- 'My son is anxious about his exams and I feel an echo of the shame and sense of failure I felt at my own mixed performance at school.'

- 'Even going into my child's school for parents' evening can seem strangely unsettling, bringing back bad memories and a tightness in my stomach dating back to my own school years.'

- 'Other parents seem naturally to form cliques while waiting at the school gates – and it reminds me of how I felt at school when I wasn't one of the "popular ones".'

- 'I feel my child isn't being treated fairly by teachers and I feel anger welling up – just as I used to when I felt dismissed by authority figures.'

As with any emotional distress, the best thing you can do for your teenager – before you say or do anything – is to pause, take five deep breaths and examine what kind of feeling is arising within you. By noticing the reaction, you can observe your anger, or your frustration or your sadness, before it spills out in words or actions that don't reflect your values. Your greater level of awareness allows you to avoid getting caught up in a vicious cycle driven by old feelings. By taking a moment before you respond, you will allow the voice of your 'inner parent' to speak.

Responding to rejection

Rejection of any kind can be painful, but being rejected by your own child can seem unbearable. All of us have 'rejection buttons' that can be pushed when a relatively trivial experience of rejection in the present brings up much rawer feelings from our past. This is likely to happen more often as your child enters the teenage years, when they will naturally want to assert their independence and test what happens when they deliberately defy you.

It may help to reflect on the fact that an angry teenager is not actually rejecting you; on the contrary, they are projecting their emotional turmoil on to you precisely because they need you. Your job is to see their reaction for what it is: the playing out of overwhelming feelings they have not yet learned to manage. It's exhausting to deal with a difficult teen on a daily basis, and sometimes you might feel as if you've simply had enough. But by learning to see *through* their drama, you can take it less personally. The one thing you can always do is take responsibility for your own feelings and try to stay as calm and centred as you can.

Indeed, the very moments when children or teenagers are pushing you away or withdrawing are the times they need you to remain as the 'safe haven' to which they will eventually return. As long as you are able to hold a steady space within yourself, they will sense it at some deep level – even if they have just stormed out of the room or refused to eat the dinner you so carefully prepared. As the parent, you have greater self-awareness, and the ability to pause and choose whether to perpetuate the cycle of acting out past hurts, or create a space for something new to take their place.

Try It: Talking about feelings

One way to help both you and your teenager manage your feelings is the simple practice of naming how you feel. Research by the neuroscientist Dr Matthew Lieberman suggests that labelling emotions activates the prefrontal cortex – the rational part of the 'upstairs' brain – and calms the 'smoke alarm' in the amygdala. Dr Daniel Siegel calls this technique 'name it to tame it'. It's also the reason why chatting to a friend about difficult feelings, writing them down or talk therapy can be so helpful.

In dealing with a difficult teenager, it is very easy to feel overwhelmed, disrespected, disappointed or upset. Such feelings are normal, but you don't have to let them control the way you respond. It can help to explain calmly to your teen how you feel about their behaviour: *'I feel really disappointed/angry/ hurt right now.'* By choosing to offer information about your feelings – rather than lashing out – you are providing your teen with a model of how to handle difficult emotions with maturity.

Some common problems

Let's take a moment to look at some of the problems I see most often in my work with teenagers. This is not meant to be a comprehensive account – rather a summary of some of the most common difficulties and the responses that often help. As with all aspects of parenting, the key is to cultivate your own ability to remain in touch with your 'inner parent'. Teens are far more likely to confide in you if they trust that you will be able to hear their distress, resist the urge to judge them or immediately jump in with advice, and move forward from a place of calm. If you feel you need additional support, then you may wish to consult your family GP.

Body image

Across Britain, teenage girls are silently battling feelings of inferiority because they do not feel they measure up to the air-brushed versions of the feminine ideal promoted by the media and the fashion industry, or the carefully filtered selfies posted by their peers. I see this problem all the time: so many girls are convinced they are too fat, too thin, too short, too tall, or they don't like their nose, thighs, freckles or hair. Some suffer from serious eating disorders, such as bulimia or anorexia, and need specialist care. (A detailed exploration of these illnesses is beyond the scope of this book – there are some suggestions for further resources on page 248.) Many others simply live with the constant nagging voice of their 'inner critic', or even the cruel voice of bullies, telling them they are weird, ugly or fat. Increasingly, teenage boys are also falling prey to similar insecurities about whether their physique conforms to the ideals they see online or on TV. The distress of young people suffering in this way is a national shame, and heartbreaking for any parent.

It's easy to feel helpless in the face of such deep, collective pain, but I've been privileged to work with teens who have learned to appreciate that their inner qualities are far more important than how they look. This isn't necessarily an easy journey to make. Many teenagers can see right through our appearance-obsessed culture, but struggle to believe they will amount to anything or achieve any worthwhile goals in a society where looks count for so much. They know deep down that they will never look like a Victoria's Secret model or a Premier League footballer – and no amount of reassurance will convince them that they're good enough. As one teenage girl said to me, 'It's all very well saying I'm a kind, fun person to be around – but boys my age want someone who looks like Selena Gomez.' Indeed, it might not help to try to cheer up a teenage girl who's convinced she is ugly by saying, 'No you're not, you're so pretty.' Such a comment may be well intentioned, but it reinforces the idea that being 'pretty' is what matters most.

I try to help teens dig deeper and discover they are more powerful than they realize. By identifying their strengths and starting to pursue their dreams more fully, they can project an inner confidence that shines more brightly than any of the Photoshopped images they see in magazines. It can help to acknowledge the darker side of the fashion industry – and that many of the celebrities teenagers worship are going through their own struggles behind the glossy façade. Without needing to become harsh or aggressive, teenage girls can start to value their potential to grow into strong women who stand up for what they believe in, regardless of what anyone else might think. They can learn to appreciate their bodies less in terms of their looks and more in terms of health and vitality. Such changes will unfold more quickly when a parent can model the kind of self-acceptance they would wish for their child.

The problem for many parents is that they themselves have spent a lifetime battling an 'inner critic' who is similarly focused on their body-shape, and they may have struggled with their own relationship to food. As we saw in Session 3, the more we notice the 'inner critic' at work, the less influence it has over us. By learning to accept our own appearance, we can help our teenagers do the same. We can gradually create an environment that encourages them to adopt a more expansive view of themselves than the degree to which they might resemble Justin Bieber or Taylor Swift.

Here are some of the approaches I use when working with teenagers and their families where body image is an issue:

- **Mindful speech.** We refrain from complimenting appearance in favour of praising qualities such as kindness, how a teenager treats others or the effort they've put into something. Better to downplay the importance of looks altogether and focus on the inner strengths that allow a teen to contribute to the lives of their friends, family and community. We try to live by the same values, and become more aware of the potential message we may inadvertently send when we compare our own looks unfavourably with other people, or glance in the mirror and mutter, 'Ugh, I need to lose a few pounds.'

- **Praise vitality rather than appearance.** Rather than telling a teen how beautiful or good-looking they are, focus on their vitality or inner glow. I sometimes say to a teenager, 'Something is shining through you today.' It also helps if adults refrain from commenting too much on other people's appearance to avoid reinforcing the idea that looks are all-important.

- **Honest conversations.** Teens can seem so worldly in some respects that it's easy to forget that they may not fully appreciate realities that may be obvious to adults: the celebrities they admire are portrayed in carefully doctored images and accompanied by armies of personal trainers, beauticians, nutritionists and cosmetic surgeons – they are not living normal lives.

- **Discuss healthy eating and exercise.** It may be obvious to adults, but many teens don't grasp the importance of a balanced diet at this crucial time for the development of their body and brain. It can also help if the whole family adopts healthier routines in terms of exercise and diet, with a focus on feeling wholesome and energized rather than measuring weight.

- **Men have a role.** It's important for dads or other male relatives to play their part in supporting teenage girls and boys to appreciate their inner qualities and see through the illusions peddled by the advertising industry. Young men need role models who can show them that being a man is not about conforming to macho stereotypes or succumbing to peer pressure, but learning to trust their own judgement and respect themselves and others, particularly in the way they relate to women.

It's not easy to help teenagers stand apart from the corrosive aspects of our culture. Ultimately, the most important thing is to show them that the values they bring into the world in the way they live their lives are far more important than how they look.

Exam stress

Teenagers can feel an enormous amount of pressure at exam time, and they may well be moody or irritable, or seem overwhelmed. It's natural for any parent to want their child to achieve good grades. However, anxiety can quickly spread, so it's important to try to keep your cool even if your teen is feeling the strain. It can be comforting to remember that if your child is worried about their grades, at least it shows they care. Take five deep breaths to connect to the part of yourself that loves your child regardless of how they perform.

When discussing exam stress with your teen, try to address specific issues that are bothering them, normalize their feelings and find out the best practical ways in which you can support them. Helping them find a suitable study space is obviously important, whether they enjoy silence or prefer to work with music or television in the background. Some teens may want to be left largely to their own devices, others may appreciate you showing solidarity by bringing them snacks and drinks when they are up late studying. By providing a kind, nurturing presence, you can model the kind of self-care that will serve them well in later life.

Providing heartfelt praise for the effort they put in is important too. It's easy to forget that teenagers need to feel those expressions of delight over the determination they show that we may have more easily expressed when they were little ones.

Here are some more tips:

● **Give them a break.** You may wish to review the chores or Saturday jobs teens normally do and recognize that they might be a bit grumpier or snappier than usual. Feeling stressed over GCSEs or A-levels is normal.

● **Reassurance.** Make sure your teen knows you will love them regardless of their grades, and that life is full of opportunities, whatever results they obtain. Teens can feel a paralysing fear of letting down their parents, teachers or themselves. Help them put things in perspective and challenge any tendency to catastrophize.

- **Mini-rewards.** We can forget that the prospect of a few months of revision can seem like a lifetime to a teen. Keep reminding them that exam season isn't for ever, and that each piece of work they complete takes them a step closer to the finish line. Help them to schedule mini-rewards along the way, and talk about things they have to look forward to when it's all done.

Kim: 'I'll be happy if you do your best'

'My fifteen-year-old daughter, Amber, has no self-confidence and she's always talking about how she doesn't feel good enough. She doesn't like how she looks and now she's barely eating because she thinks she's fat – which she isn't. It breaks my heart that Amber feels like this. She's a perfectionist and she's determined to get into a good university. I don't put her under any pressure, but the teachers are pretty pushy at her school, and to be honest I think the other girls work each other up about their results. I tell her I'll be happy if she just does her best – but she doesn't see it like that. She feels that if she doesn't get it "right" now, she will have screwed up the rest of her life. There seems to be so much more pressure these days. It wasn't like that when I was young. We had no idea what we were going to do with the rest of our lives. I wouldn't have had a clue. I keep telling Amber that her well-being is the most important thing, but she says that's easy for me to say as I'm not the one taking my GCSEs. They were told at school that they aren't just competing with the others in the class – they are competing with every child in the country. It's a pressure I just couldn't believe.'

Anxiety and panic attacks

A certain amount of worry or nervousness is normal – it's what keeps us sharp. But for anybody who has never experienced a severe form of anxiety, it can be hard to grasp just how debilitating the condition can be. What starts as a background feeling of dread can rapidly spiral into a crippling fear that can leave a teenager afraid to take on simple tasks such as speaking in class, hanging out with friends or attending a family gathering. In some cases, anxiety can erupt into a full-blown panic attack – accompanied by sweating, a racing heart, hyperventilation and palpitations. The attack may last only a few minutes, but the fear can be so intense that sufferers can be convinced they are about to die.

Fortunately, there is a lot that can be done to help teenagers suffering from anxiety – the most common mental health problem among the under-eighteens. It can occur in a number of forms, from social anxiety and phobias to Obsessive Compulsive Disorder, so it's worth finding out which form a teen may be experiencing. There are many helpful organizations, online resources and books to help parents and teenagers understand and address these conditions (see Resources, pages 242–4).

In my work with families, I often encounter teenagers suffering from social anxiety. Whilst a degree of self-consciousness is normal in teens, some become so awkward and preoccupied with their fears of being judged as weird, stupid, boring, ugly or fat that it's not an exaggeration to say that they can barely function. They are desperate to fit in, but feel they don't belong. In some cases, this unease can escalate into a panic attack. If this happens to your teen, here are a few points to bear in mind about what's going on – and how to respond:

- **Over-reaction.** Panic attacks happen when the body's fight-or-flight response has been triggered. The amygdala – the brain's 'smoke alarm' – is reacting as if you are in mortal danger, even though you aren't. This can create an overwhelming feeling of fear which can come on suddenly and last for about ten or fifteen minutes (although it may seem like much longer).

- **Catastrophic thinking.** The mind is misinterpreting the physical sensations that accompany anxiety as a sign of impending catastrophe. Teenagers suffering a panic attack may fear they are going to faint or suffer a heart attack.

- **Empathize.** Even if you've never had a panic attack yourself, don't underestimate how distressing they can be for your teen. Their brain is convinced they are facing mortal danger, even if they are completely safe.

- **Identify triggers.** Panic attacks are usually triggered by a certain situation, such as having to speak in front of class or taking exams. Discuss with your teen whether they occur at specific times of day, such as late at night, when they are tired and feeling stressed about school the next day.

- **Soothe them.** During an attack, speak as calmly as possible and remain as centred as you can, perhaps by taking five deep breaths. Remind them that anxiety is a normal response (designed to prepare the body for danger) and that they have come through this before. Consider placing a calm picture – something they have chosen – in their room or on their phone. Remind them to take five deep breaths too.

- **Agree on a response.** Figure out with your teen what would be most helpful for them if they are gripped by a panic attack and agree on a course of action in advance. Would they like you to remain with them, offering comforting comments or a rub on the back? Or would they prefer to be left alone? Perhaps going for a walk or exercising can help release the build-up of excess energy. It's important to agree on how you can respond to these attacks as a team.

As always, the key thing when confronted with a teen in distress is to remain as calm as possible and provide the safe haven they need to feel secure.

Self-harm

Most common among teenage girls, self-harm usually involves some form of cutting arms or legs, usually with razor blades, though sometimes with knives, scissors or pins – or burning with cigarette lighters. There are usually strong feelings of secrecy, guilt and shame attached, and teens often fear telling parents because they feel they've let them down and that they won't understand.

Teenagers may feel very reluctant to confide in you, but they need to know that if they do try to talk to you they won't be judged, and that you can cope with what you're hearing. This isn't always easy: it's natural that self-harm can bring up a strong mix of feelings, and it can be hard to comprehend how or why a young person could do this to themselves. In their distress, many parents naturally fear that their child's self-harming is evidence that they want to take their own life. Although self-harm *can* be a risk factor for suicide, in the vast majority of cases I've seen the young person has no intention of killing themselves. They are usually trying to cope with intense emotions, and may even have been exposed to social media sites that romanticize self-harm. The behaviour becomes easier to understand when you consider that the brain circuits involved in physical pain are very closely related to those that govern emotional pain, so cutting can provide a temporary feeling of relief. These young people need help to find better ways to manage their feelings and become more emotionally resilient.

The best thing you can do when faced with such a situation is to nurture yourself as far as possible and be the non-judgemental, safe parent that your teen can open up to. Talking about it will not make it worse; it will provide a space where your teen can begin to explore their feelings.

Here are some additional pointers some parents find helpful:

- **Keep talking.** Since self-harm is often cloaked in strong feelings of shame, it's important to strike a balance between keeping a dialogue going and ensuring you don't put your child under too much pressure, which could make them even more secretive.

● **Identify triggers.** Talk with your child to find out what kinds of stressors make them more likely to self-harm – for example: arguments with friends, feelings of rejection, stresses over schoolwork, or bullying on social media.

● **Healthier outlets.** Help your child to find other ways to manage their unwanted feelings, such as exercise, writing, breathing, trampolining or playing an instrument. Encourage them to experiment with substitutes for self-harm, such as squeezing stress balls, pinging an elastic band on a wrist, drawing on an arm in red pen, screaming into a pillow or throwing socks against a wall. See if they can distract themselves from their urge to self-harm by setting a timer for ten minutes, using music or YouTube, or phoning a friend.

● **Seek support.** There are many groups, online resources and books for parents facing self-harm, and it may be that you and your child need professional support. (See Resources, page 250.)

Depression

Characterized by a persistent low mood, sadness and a general sense of apathy, depression is usually accompanied by a loss of interest in activities a teen usually enjoys. Sufferers may become withdrawn and spend a lot of time alone in their room. You may notice that they are self-critical, tearful, tired and often yawning a lot because they are having difficulty sleeping. They may also be irritable and suffer angry outbursts, and either lose their appetite or binge-eat. They may feel hopeless or suicidal and say things like, 'I wish it would all end.'

Sometimes it can be very difficult to tell the difference between a teenager who is going through a period of withdrawal or moodiness and somebody who is suffering from depression. Some teenagers become adept at hiding their chronic unhappiness because they fear being stigmatized or further alienated, or they may not want to be a burden on their families and friends. They may also be reluctant to seek help because they fear they are beyond hope and feel very alone. This is understandably very worrying for parents, particularly when you feel you can't get through to them. It's vitally important that a teenager suffering in this way finds somebody they can open up to. It may be that you will need to help them access professional help by consulting your GP. (For an excellent online resource on depression, see YoungMinds on page 244.)

Sex and relationships

Young people will at some point start experimenting with their sexuality and dating. Although this is natural and inevitable, it can still be difficult as a parent to acknowledge that your teen is growing up. As with other issues confronting your teen, the key is to start a conversation about what makes a healthy relationship as soon as you feel they're ready. It goes without saying that some teens may find having these kinds of discussions with their parents excruciatingly embarrassing, but it's important to try to connect: you can provide vital information on the risks and responsibilities that sexual activity brings, and offer a mature perspective on what it means to respect yourself and others in relationships.

This is an emotive topic and it can bring up powerful feelings, especially if you feel your teen is putting themselves at risk or disrespecting you. As a parent, it's obviously important to set appropriate limits to keep your teen safe. If these boundaries are breached, try not to over-react, as this will only push your teen away and shut communication down. The more you can step back from your reactions, the greater your ability to ensure your teen feels heard, no matter how shocked you may feel. You can't control the decisions your teen will make about sex, but you can choose how to respond. If you can approach the situation calmly, you'll have a much better chance of working together to help your teen develop the maturity they will need to make good decisions – now and in the future.

Friendships

While the dramas of classroom friendships may seem trifling compared to adult concerns, the emotional stakes can be very real for teenagers. It can be heart-rending as a parent to see your lovely daughter suddenly being ostracized for no apparent reason, or obsessed by the belief that her friends are much prettier or more popular, or to see your gentle son being mercilessly bullied – face-to-face or online. Teenagers can be very cruel, blanking each other or dishing out verbal abuse that can be as painful as physical blows.

The challenge is to know when to get involved and when to hold back. Friendships offer vital opportunities for teens to learn to resolve conflicts, assert themselves and learn social skills that will be vital in adult life. Intervening too much can deprive them of these lessons. The most helpful thing is to provide a listening ear and gently help a teen see that often their friends' behaviour says a lot more about them. You can ask whether somebody who is happy would behave in such a nasty way, and help a teenager to see that whilst the 'popular ones' may appear to have many friends, it doesn't mean they are the most likeable people. Explain that bullies resort to their horrible behaviour to give them a feeling of being in control, often because they are hiding deep feelings of fear, anger or shame.

I have found that with a little encouragement some children and teens can come up with imaginative inner resources that help bolster their confidence. For example, I have worked with young people of different ages who use a variety of visualizations to feel 'protected' at school:

- **Shields, armour and force fields.** A mask that shoots out a force field of protection. An invisible bubble. Ivy vines that erupt and absorb unkind words. Medieval-style armour or shields.

- **Imaginary headphones.** To block out harsh comments. The wearer repeats the mantra: 'That's just their opinion – it doesn't make it true.'

- **Angel wings.** To bat away negative comments.

It can also be helpful to talk to a teen about being assertive rather than accepting bullying passively or lashing out in response. (See Resources, page 246.)

The role of mentors

In sensitive teenage years, it's normal for an adolescent to be shy or embarrassed about opening up to their parents. It can be invaluable for a teen to develop a relationship with a 'mentor' figure – perhaps an aunt or uncle, a godparent or other family friend. Teens may feel more comfortable opening up about their problems to somebody slightly removed from their immediate family – and that's not a sign of failure on the part of the parent. As Steve Biddulph, the Australian family therapist, observes: it's often easier to speak to other people's children than our own.

*

The five key points

Surviving the teenage years

- Teens go through a lot: don't forget to celebrate their gifts.

- Crises will pass quicker if you can work through them calmly.

- Control or lectures won't work: teens respond to trust and respect.

- Teenage brains are different: try not to take their behaviour too personally.

- Your connection will yo-yo: let your teen know you're always there.

In the land of the 'diginatives'

It's not so long since mobile phones were the stuff of science fiction. Today, a six-year-old armed with a smartphone wields more computing power than NASA marshalled to land astronauts on the moon. No previous generation of parents has been forced to confront the implications of such a profound technological shift for their 'diginatives' – the first humans to grow up surrounded by mobile devices from birth. The technology has opened up undreamed-of worlds to young people, allowing them to inform and educate themselves in ways that we would have found unimaginable, and to forge diverse friendships that span the globe.

For all these wonderful benefits, the technology is still so new that there is no consensus on what impact it may have or how best to handle it. One day we are being warned of the dangers tablets may pose to young attention spans, only for another study to suggest that computer games enhance problem-solving skills. We may wonder whether there is a 'right' age for children to start using devices and worry about the consequences of excessive screen time on maturing brains. We might also be concerned about cyber-bullying, or possible exposure to online grooming or porn. In this new territory, there are no ready-made answers and it's easy to feel others are judging the choices we make. Traditional parent–child roles are reversed as we – the adults – find ourselves struggling to keep up with tech-savvy sons and daughters vanishing down the trail into a digital forest.

Take heart: just as parents have always had to take responsibility for a child's nutrition, twenty-first-century mums and dads are learning to oversee their youngsters' digital lives. You don't have to be on top of the latest mobile apps or developments in gaming technology to be up to the task. Today's parents are fortunate enough to remember that a world existed before the advent of mobile technology, so we can see its many facets with greater perspective than the 'diginatives', who have never known life without smartphones. Our job is not to serve as digital police, but to help children use the rational, decision-making parts of their 'upstairs' brain to reflect on their relationship with technology so they can enjoy the benefits while avoiding the pitfalls. Different children will react to technology in different ways: some may be naturally adept at making their devices work for them, others more prone to falling into an addictive relationship with their screens. With no hard-and-fast rules to follow, this is especially fertile territory for consulting your 'inner parent'.

As with every parental challenge, the most important first step is to ensure that you are acting from a place of calm and stillness within yourself. Whenever a challenge arises, there is always the possibility of pausing, dropping your attention into your body and taking five deep breaths. In this session I share a number of ways of approaching digital dilemmas that have emerged through my own work with families and the insights from others who have also confronted this issue. I also look at handling specific problems – from the increasingly common phenomenon of cyber-bullying, to online porn and sexting. In all cases, several key principles apply:

- **A continuous conversation.** It's never too early to start talking about how to make the best of the online world while minimizing the risks. Conversations should ideally start as soon as your child is old enough to search the internet or use YouTube, and you can revisit these chats as often as needed. Try to strike a casual tone rather than turning the subject into a big deal, which could put your child on edge.

● **Keep an eye on the computer.** If possible, locate the computer your child uses in a central area of the home where you can keep a discreet eye on what they are doing. Familiarize yourself with privacy settings and parental controls – while remaining mindful of children's frequent aptitude for unlocking security systems and guessing passwords. It will be harder to monitor smartphone or tablet use in the same way, which is why an open dialogue is so important.

● **Manage your reaction.** Remember to pay attention to what's going on for you when your child runs into online problems. Take five deep breaths, even as you acknowledge the reality of the distress your child may be experiencing, whether it be from cyber-bullying or other forms of abuse. Offload any upset you may feel with your partner or a friend rather than in front of your child.

● **Confiscate as a last resort.** If your child fears you may take away their device, they are less likely to tell you if they run into problems online.

● **Seek solutions together.** Use any online difficulties as opportunities to help your child develop their own problem-solving skills. There are many excellent websites to help parents and children to manage their online lives which you can work through together. (Some suggestions can be found in Resources, pages 247–8.)

● **Encourage children to think before they post.** It's not easy for impulsive teens to exercise self-restraint online, but the more you can maintain a dialogue with them about the importance of considering the impact of each status update, text and photo they send, the more likely they are to employ good judgement.

● **Emphasize the positives.** Young people love the online world and they will respond if you show an interest in the positive aspects of their experience. Ask them about the connections they make with friends, the new perspectives they gain on issues, the interests they pursue and the games they enjoy.

You and your phone

I've found that before parents begin to formulate specific plans for managing their children's use of technology, they often find it helpful to consider their own relationship with their devices. If we can manage our own phone use in an optimal way, our children are far more likely to follow suit.

It's no secret that phones are beautifully addictive. How many of us find ourselves idly scrolling while waiting at the check-out or at the bus stop, or instinctively checking our email as soon as we wake up? According to some counts, the average person checks their phone 110 times a day. Certainly, I've noticed that if I've got a bit of time to myself I can easily fritter it away on my smartphone. None of us needs reminding that it's easy to spend time immersed in a phone that might have been better spent appreciating our surroundings or chatting to a friend. Nevertheless, it can be helpful to reflect a little further on what role our devices play in our lives. Here are some of the kinds of questions some parents find it helpful to explore:

● How easily can I sit still without feeling an urge to check my phone?

● Do I check my phone because I need to, or because the distraction helps take the edge off boredom or anxiety?

● I hear a tone alerting me to a new message. Do I finish what I'm doing and check it later? Or do I feel compelled to check it immediately?

- When I meet up with somebody, do I place the phone on the table between us or stow it out of sight in a coat or bag?

- Does frequent phone-checking ever cause tension in my family?

- When watching any form of live event, do I often find myself recording it on my phone rather than enjoying the moment?

- When was the last time I went out without my phone?

- When was the last time I was in a different room from my phone?

- How often do I give my child my undivided attention without pausing midway through a conversation to send a text or check my phone?

- How often am I spending time with my child without my phone in my hand?

- Do I often video or take pictures of special moments with my child instead of being fully present as they happen?

As we learn to live more in the moment, mindfulness helps us to notice the effect our phones may be having on us. We become more aware of the way the ping of a new text message or a notification on Facebook tugs at our attention, demanding an instant response. As we see our habitual reactions with greater clarity, we can choose to pause and decide whether we need to check the phone straight away or stay with what we're doing and leave it for later. As always, tuning in to the sensations in our body, and noticing our breath, serves to bring us back to the here and now. By focusing our attention in this way, we make space for our 'inner parent' to speak.

The pleasures and perils of social media

In the space of only a few years, it has become hard to imagine what life would be like without Facebook, Twitter and Instagram. Many parents I speak to use their Facebook page or parenting blogs as lifelines where they can draw on the support of a like-minded community whose amusing posts or reassuring comments can be an invaluable boost after a tough day. Social media can be a source of practical advice, inspiration or support, and above all can remind us that we're not alone – especially if we are looking after kids and craving some adult company. A few minutes absorbed on our favourite sites can feel like well-deserved down time.

Nevertheless, for all these benefits, some parents report that their experiences are not always entirely positive. Much as it can be rewarding to keep up to date with our friends' news, if we're feeling a little low ourselves then we might be more vulnerable to experiencing a stab of envy as we scroll through pictures of beach holidays, children's parties or meals out. It can sometimes feel as if the carefully selected images have been filtered in some mysterious way to highlight the very areas where we feel a sense of lack in our lives. Indeed, one mother sparked newspaper headlines when she wrote in desperation that Facebook would be better named 'BeatYourselfUpBook'. On the other hand, we may be such enthusiastic contributors of images and updates to our own feeds that we find it increasingly difficult to enjoy a special dinner or a walk in the park for its own sake, rather than living in constant anticipation of a deluge of comments and likes that will follow when we post documentary evidence on our wall.

We should also be aware of what exactly it is we're sharing when we post. Bear in mind that many digital photos contain what is known as 'geo-location' data that reveals exactly where a picture was taken. You can adjust the settings on a camera or camera app to reduce the amount of this hidden 'meta-data' in each photo to ensure you are not putting more information than may be wise into the public domain. It's also possible that some children may object when they eventually discover how much of their early lives has effectively been turned into public property. In this age of 'sharenting', more and more parents are starting to question the wisdom of posting so much of their children's lives online, where images and updates can form a permanent 'digital tattoo'.

If you feel you want to explore your own relationship with social media more deeply, here are some of the sorts of questions you might wish to consider:

- How much time do I spend on social media each day?

- Do I check social media first thing in the morning? Last thing at night?

- Do I use social media as a form of entertainment?

- How often do I turn to social media to soothe myself when I feel stressed?

- What kinds of feelings do I experience as I scroll through other people's updates?

- How often am I drawn into arguments on comment pages?

- When I see a notification, do I feel compelled to check it immediately?

- How much do I know about the way the images I share of my children could potentially be accessed and reproduced by strangers?

- Do I focus on body image: how my friends look? Celebrity pictures?

- Do I find myself monitoring the number of 'likes' my posts receive? Or hoping to receive more comments?

- If I post something and I get only a few 'likes', do I feel disappointed?

- Is my absorption in social media causing me to miss out on opportunities to interact with my child and partner?

These questions do not have right or wrong answers. They are merely tools for looking more closely at your relationship with social media so that you can confidently model the kind of behaviour you'd like to see reflected by your child.

Staying safe online

There was a time when parents wondered how best to broach the subject of the birds and the bees. These days, mums and dads are facing up to the necessity of having equivalent conversations with their children about the risks they might face online. Lecturing or trying to instil fear rarely works – children are far more likely to respond to a conversation where you are curious about what they think.

All families are facing similar challenges, and you are not alone when it comes to your concerns about safety. Parents confront a real dilemma. You may want to introduce boundaries on online activity, but on the other hand you don't want to undermine your child's ability to make the most of the internet or to socialize with other children who are not subject to the same limits. We may worry about the amount of time our child spends online – but if all his friends are doing the same, will he be left out or even exposed to bullying or ridicule if we make our own rules?

Screen time – how much is too much?

Newborn babies are likely to have their first encounter with a screen when their picture is snapped shortly after they've left the womb. Many toddlers start swiping at tablets before they reach their first birthday, and young children soon learn to play games or watch clips on YouTube.

Growing numbers of studies are trying to assess the potential impact of screens on child development, but the technology is so new that it's too early to draw firm conclusions. Some researchers have questioned whether too much screen time or television may hinder a toddler's capacity to bond with adult care-givers – though what parent hasn't plonked their kids in front of a TV or iPad from time to time, just for a moment's peace, to make space for a chat with a friend or to guarantee a stress-free plane journey? That welcome respite may be what helps you to get through the day.

Managing devices can often be so hard because they seem to stimulate the reward system in the brain – meaning it's very easy for a child's 'downstairs' brain to become activated when they are suddenly deprived of their screen, which can lead to explosive results. Tablets may seem like great pacifiers for young children, but it's essential that they learn to cope without constant digital stimulation. If young children can't sit still without a screen to distract them, they won't learn to manage their emotions, leaving them more vulnerable to mood swings and tantrums as they grow up.

With parents often adopting very different approaches, it's tempting to worry that our own policy is either too lax or too harsh, and we may feel criticized no matter what we do. Part of the answer may be to focus less on arbitrary rules and more on forming a positive vision of what your family wants to get out of digital technology and the kinds of drawbacks you want to avoid. For example, you may wish to make agreements about certain times when phones are switched off to encourage family members to talk to one another – perhaps during meals, or after a certain time of day. You might all see the value of using a tablet to help pass the time on a long car journey, but agree that if there's an opportunity to play outdoors or develop face-to-face friendships, then screens should be put away.

Finding a way to oversee screen time may seem daunting, but it can also present new opportunities to forge a deeper connection. Given the lack of any established formula, this is an ideal arena to tune in to your own guidance and trust what feels right for you.

Trolls, hate sites and 'roasting'

Cyber-bullying is by far the biggest problem affecting young people online. It can take many forms: trolling with vicious posts on social media; excluding individuals from online social groups or games; pressure to send naked selfies or engage in 'sexting'; the posting of embarrassing personal details, pictures or videos; setting up 'hate sites' or digitally blanking somebody by refusing to like or comment on their status updates or photos. Girls can often be the victims, but there are also growing numbers of teenage boys subjected to 'roasting' – nasty online attacks by gangs of female peers. Sometimes this can be an extension of bullying at school, or it can be anonymous and even conducted through the use of fake accounts. As one mother put it to me: at least in the old days bullying only took place during school hours. In the age of cyber-bullying, it can feel like there's no escape.

It may not always be obvious if your child is being subjected to cyber-bullying, though any indication that they are feeling sad or anxious while online can be a tell-tale sign. The public nature of social media can make the target feel as if a situation is rapidly spiralling out of control. As a parent, the most important thing is to monitor your own reaction before responding. However angry or upset you feel, the best thing you can do for your child is to remain calm and work with them to agree the best course of action. For example, it's important to acknowledge the depth of the hurt they may be experiencing and ensure they feel heard. Try to avoid any variation of the 'sticks and stones may break my bones but words will never hurt me' speech: for children suffering online abuse, the wounds are all too real.

As you work through the options with your child, it's worth bearing in mind that in the online world the distinction between victim and perpetrator can easily blur. Children who engage in cyber-bullying may once have been victims themselves, and vice-versa. It's often best to resist the impulse to confront culprits or their parents immediately and instead work with your child on how to respond. However, if your child is being subjected to consistent abuse or threats online it may be wise to consult school authorities or the police. Keep screenshots of offensive material, save nasty messages and bear in mind that in some cases cyber-bullying can be a crime.

Kevin: 'It's hard enough being a teenager'

'As if being a teenager isn't difficult enough, they now have every single one of their embarrassing moments posted on social media. Every argument or falling out – it's all shared so publicly. It's torturous. Sometimes I just wish I could take the kids away to a quiet, secluded island with no technology so they could play outside and enjoy these years without any hassle or threats.

'My eldest daughter, Jodie, was telling me the other day there's a girl basically bullying her on Facebook. She's been posting really nasty things about her. Some of the language is pretty revolting – they've called her a "slut" and all sorts of horrible things. As a dad, you just don't know what to do. You can't stop your kids using social media – but it's very difficult to prevent it getting out of hand.'

Onscreen friendships

For today's 'screenagers', the internet can be a great way to expand their circle of friends and learn the value of cooperation and kindness online. For children who are shy or have difficulty socializing, online connections can be genuine lifelines. Nevertheless, friendships mediated through screens bring new risks – from the ease with which bullies can single out their victims on social media, to the dangers inherent in interacting with strangers.

I have been struck by the number of parents I have seen whose distraught children have discovered that social media has amplified the effects of the fickle friendships, insecurities over appearance and bullying that have traditionally marked turbulent teenage years. It is all too easy for teenagers grappling with difficult emotions or trying to fit in to share more in their posts than might be wise. It is perhaps not surprising that the high drama unfolding over messaging apps in hours-long exchanges can make for late nights and prove far more compelling than homework. Teenagers simply don't want to miss out on what's going on, whatever the time of day. As one teenage girl confessed to me with unabashed frankness, 'It's just more fun looking at my phone than studying. I need to constantly check in with my friends to make sure they still like me, and that I'm not missing out on anything.'

Sex, selfies and self-harm

For many teenage girls, sites such as Facebook and Instagram have become arenas where they feel obliged to spend hours snapping selfies at just the right angle and manipulating the resulting images to maximum effect. They often post pictures that make them appear far more mature than they actually are. Parents may rightfully worry about the representation of women online, when so much of the media is obsessed by surgically enhanced celebrities rather than examples of inspiring, strong role models. Likewise, with the prevalence of self-harm among teenagers rising, it's increasingly easy to find fellow self-harmers online who normalize and may even encourage the behaviour – a phenomenon which many parents understandably find incomprehensible and shocking. (For more on self-harm, see Session 8 and also Resources, page 250.)

Similarly, 'sexting' and the sending of nude selfies have become increasingly common among teenagers. Most young people don't see sexting as a problem and are understandably reluctant to discuss it with adults. For parents, it's important to maintain a continuous dialogue. You can use something you're watching on TV or a film, images on a billboard glimpsed during a car journey, or a story in the news to kick-start a casual chat about sexuality. You could also mention you've been having a conversation about teenage sexting with another parent and ask your teen what they think.

Porn

It's an unpalatable reality to confront, but the fact is that virtually every child is going to stumble across porn online. Young people are naturally curious about sex, and the sheer quantity of porn on the internet means that it's only a matter of time before they find illicit images, whether intentionally or by clicking on a seemingly innocent link that redirects them to a pornographic site.

The extreme nature of many of these images means they are obviously totally inappropriate for young people, and it's important to try to establish an honest dialogue with your child about what they might encounter online. The Thinkuknow website has a wealth of age-appropriate guidance to help you with these kinds of conversations. (See page 248 for more on Thinkuknow.) It's good to emphasize that it's natural for young people to be curious, but that porn is never a realistic representation of a loving relationship, and is comprised of scenes posed by actors working in a seedy industry rife with exploitation. Reassure your child that you would prefer them to tell you if they click on something they find disturbing and that they won't be in trouble.

If you do discover your child or teen is deliberately perusing porn online, measure your reaction carefully. You may be angry and disappointed, but it's important not to shame a young person – they will be embarrassed enough as it is. Instead, try to engage them in a dialogue about the values involved in a loving and authentic intimate relationship. It's worth remembering that just as only a small minority of children suffer any form of lasting harm from alcohol or drugs, the same holds true for porn.

Video games

There is a wealth of research on the impact of video games on children, but it can be very hard to find experts speaking with a single voice. The key question is what impact games seem to be having on *your* child. If long hours spent on an Xbox seem to plunge them into a trance-like state that leaves them restless and agitated, or triggers a meltdown when they are told to switch off, then it may be time to have a conversation about agreeing some limits. Help your child tune in to their body. How do they feel when they stop playing? Are they tense? Is their heart beating faster? Do they feel irritable or upset? Encourage them to rate themselves on the kind of 'anger thermometer' discussed in Session 7. You can work with your child to help them learn to regulate their own emotions as you work together to agree boundaries.

Surveillance or trust?

Technology has brought the tension society faces between the values of personal freedom and the promise of security from a 'Big Brother'-style state into our homes. There are now growing numbers of apps and other devices that can be used to monitor or restrict a child's online activity. There is no doubt that some form of parental control is essential to keep youngsters safe online. However, the ultimate insurance policy is a HEART-centred connection with your child that will encourage them to listen to you and have the confidence to confide in you if things go wrong. Relying too heavily on technological fixes as opposed to honest conversations can send a tacit message that you don't trust them. It's far better to nurture a relationship of mutual respect. (For more resources, see pages 247–8.)

Connecting across a console

Though you might not have much interest in games, you can have a go at using them as an opportunity to connect by asking your child to show you how to play, even for a few minutes. Your predictably abysmal performance will be a guaranteed source of amusement. At a deeper level, children enjoy any situation of role reversal where they gain temporary, safe power over adults: part of the reason young kids love hide-and-seek so much is that it places them in a temporary position of dominance as they hunt down a helpless parent who is only nominally 'hidden'. Similarly, computer games can elevate your child into a position of authority and cast you in the role of apprentice.

Here are some more suggestions for ways in which you can use technology to connect:

- **Rite of passage.** Entrusting a child with a phone or other device can be seen as an important initiation – one that can help them develop a sense of responsibility and mark their growing independence. It can be a good moment to have a fresh conversation about avoiding risks online and maximizing benefits.

- **Shared experience.** Brothers and sisters who might be prone to arguing can often set their differences aside through a shared session on a two-player game, especially when it involves standing shoulder-to-shoulder fighting off a horde of extra-terrestrials, or saving civilization from a zombie apocalypse.

- **Online etiquette.** Parents can encourage children to use the unique opportunities for meeting new people offered by the internet to practise the qualities of kindness, generosity, fairness and respect they would show to people they meet in person.

- **Crisis as opportunity.** As in any situation where a child is struggling, whether it be from the fall-out from cyber-bullying or losing sleep to the lure of the Xbox, the crisis can provide an opportunity to help a child develop a 'growth mindset' and learn to find answers for themselves.

- **Find your tribe.** Parents differ widely in their approaches to screens and the online world. Team up with friends who share a similar philosophy so that you can support each other's efforts to set appropriate limits and exchange ideas on what works.

Making contracts

One option for helping your children and teenagers to learn to regulate their use of technology is to create a formal 'contract' governing their – and your – screen time.

The idea is to sit down with them and come up with a set of agreements on the kind of boundaries that the whole family will apply to the use of devices. This sort of democratic approach allows you to demonstrate what it means to make an agreement and be accountable for your behaviour. Contracts might cover issues such as:

- The amount of time allocated to TV/playing video games/using a tablet per day.

- A 'switch off' time for devices in the evening.

- Dedicated 'digital detox' periods when everyone agrees to take a break from their devices.

- No scrolling through phones at mealtimes.

- Commitments by all the family on the parameters for their individual screen use.

- Possible consequences if the contract is not respected.

This contract can then be typed up, signed and posted on a wall. (There are a number of templates for such contracts available online – see pages 247–8.)

The advantage of such contracts is that they provide opportunities for discussion and a sense of shared commitment to making the most of technology while mitigating the downsides. As a parent, the exercise provides a chance to model the skills of empathy and discernment – guiding your children with confidence while giving them their say in a family decision. Having an explicit contract can also provide a sense of 'containment', helping both parents and children manage their concerns around devices. The process of setting the contract also allows parents to learn from their children about the way they use phone apps, games or tablets. A child feels respected and heard, while parents become more familiar with the reality of their online life.

Contracts can also help foster a sense of responsibility and accountability. For example, what would be the consequences if a phone is lost or broken – will the cost have to be reimbursed, perhaps in a token form through some set number of hours of chores? For older children, working through the real-world rules of signing contracts with a phone company may be a safe way to start introducing them to adult financial responsibilities.

Children who sign these contracts will often attempt to push the boundaries, as they will with any rule. This can be seen as part of a healthy impulse on the part of a child to explore and test the world around them. The fact you have taken the trouble to reach an agreement set down in the contract should make it easier for you to insist the rules are respected. It's important to talk through any breach to provide your child with an opportunity to problem-solve. The message parents are sending is, 'I'm here, we can get through this – let's work out how we're going to deal with it.' Ask your child the question, 'What can we do to help you to avoid doing that again in the future?'

Working through all this with kindness

The many dilemmas posed by technology mean that there are bound to be times when it is impossible to live up to the commitments that you may have set. In such moments, it's easy to begin to catastrophize over the potential impact of too much screen time, or the risks your child may be facing online. Meet these moments with gentleness and kindness for yourself, rather than finding another excuse to let your 'inner critic' off the leash. These are new challenges; we are all finding our way through them – and ultimately there is no hard-and-fast right or wrong way. It can help to remember one of the mantras from Session 3: 'I am kind to myself in this moment, and I am kind to my child.'

✳

The five key points

In the land of the 'diginatives'

- Helping a child manage technology is an essential part of modern parenting.

- Explore your own relationship with your phone to set the right example.

- Kids react differently to screens: trust your judgement on what's right.

- Educate yourself and start the conversation on screen use early.

- Work collaboratively through family meetings or by making contracts.

Session
10

Parenting as a team

However much we may wish things were different, romantic relationships are rarely straightforward. While the shared joy of parenting can be like nothing you've ever experienced before, the inevitable challenges of raising a child can strain even the strongest of partnerships. Everyone knows that child-raising places demands on time, energy and money, but you can never know what it's going to be like until you experience it. No two people adapt to the arrival of children in exactly the same way, and we may be surprised to discover that we naturally incline towards a very different parenting style to our partner. If we're in a couple, we might run into conflicts with our in-laws, while single parents must contend with the demands of going it alone, or we may be confronted with the complexities of stepfamilies.

However much you may love your partner, it's not uncommon for both parents to wish the other could provide them with more support – though it can be difficult to find a way to express these feelings without sliding into anger or blame. The strains can be particularly intense in the baby and toddler years. Sleep-deprived parents may feel that even when they do manage to snatch a moment of precious alone-time with their partner, it may be entirely consumed with practicalities. Little niggles that already existed in a relationship can be magnified by the demands that children bring. Fatigue doesn't help – and both partners may start wishing the other possessed mind-reading superpowers since they are too tired even to ask for more help.

The journey to having children can unfold in many different ways and can leave a legacy of strong feelings, which as a couple you may not have had time or space to process. Many women suffer miscarriages, but it can be difficult to find ways to open up about the grief and other emotions they can stir up. Undergoing fertility treatment can put additional pressures on couples, as can choosing to go down the adoption route.

As your children grow, it's easy to slip into blame mode when a child acts up or runs into problems. Memories of our more romantic early days may begin to fade as we run a constant relay race, hurriedly passing our child back and forth as we dash out to catch our train to work, drop the children off at the childminder or nursery, or juggle the school run. Life can seem like one long rush from one place to the next and we may even start to feel as though we're living with a stranger or wonder whether we're with the right person. With so much focus going into the children, maintaining our relationship inevitably takes second place.

Though these sorts of dilemmas are very common, we may find it easier to talk about the trouble we may be having with our children than confess to a friend that we're barely on speaking terms with our partner. It's easy to fall into a pattern where both parents are tired of the way snide remarks, circular rows and heavy silences or passive-aggressive behaviour have begun to define their daily lives – but neither side can see a way out of the rut. We can end up feeling that we're struggling alone, and we may harbour feelings of failure for not living up to our image of how we imagined our lives as parents and partners. As one mum put it, 'I'm the worst mum in the world – my kids are so wonderful and they deserve more than this. I may have chosen a bad relationship, but they shouldn't have to suffer. I'm so ashamed of myself.'

For much of this book, we've focused on how mindfulness can help you forge a closer HEART-centred connection with your child. In this final session, we draw together what we have learned to help you to do the same with your partner, particularly in the context of the changes that children bring. Many families do not fit the conventional pattern familiar fifty years ago, and this can create a great deal of confusion and misplaced guilt. Whatever our circumstances, bringing more awareness to our relationships can lead us to greater clarity and confidence, and help us to reveal our vulnerabilities without fear.

Heidi: 'I feel taken for granted'

'We used to be so romantic. The other day I found some letters and cards we had written to each other before we had children. We were so nice to each other – now I feel like a different person. I don't even have the time to write a few sentences to him to say loving things. I barely remember being like that.

'Conversations are always very practical. No romance. But then I feel guilty about doing anything else other than looking after the children. I even feel guilty spending money on myself.

'When my husband gets home, he feels resentful towards me as he has been working so hard, and I feel resentful towards him because I've been working just as hard as he has. So as soon as he walks in the door, I start bombarding him with what I've been doing.

'When you go to a nine-to-five job, there's a lot of praise: "Well done, tick that off the list, you've handed in the project." You don't get the same reward for being a mum. There's no one there to say, "Well done."

'If I have had a bad day with the children, I will hold it all in and then take it out on him when he gets home. I get jealous of him: jealous of his commute and the silent, quiet time he gets standing on the platform of the train station. The other day I had a meltdown. My *husband was away and I had PMT. The kids were all hanging off me; I felt bedraggled and harassed as I took them to school.*

'One of the other mothers must have noticed as she asked me, "Are you okay?" I said, "I feel like a slave." This mum said to me, "You are a slave!" She totally empathized with how I was feeling in that moment. It really helped to talk to someone who understood.'

Towards a new way of relating

We've all grown up absorbing myths about love and marriage that teach us that the perfect partner is all we need to make us happy. In reality, we know that life doesn't work that way. We all have to take responsibility for our own inner state: we can't expect another person to manage our feelings for us, no matter how much we may love them or however attractive they may be. As long as we're waiting for somebody else to 'complete' us, we will be disappointed again and again. The more you look to your partner for fulfilment, the more frustrated you will get. Only once we've found the source of peace, joy and contentment within ourselves can we start to share these qualities with someone else.

Faced with the challenges of parenting, it's only natural to hope your partner will do everything they can to help you feel better when you are struggling – and it's wonderful when they do. But there will inevitably be times when our partners do not live up to our expectations and we feel our needs are not being met. It's easy to feel that we are missing out on the love and support we deserve, and we may start to take our disappointment and resentment out on our partner. We may imagine that things would be different if only they'd make more of an effort, or if they'd followed our ideas about parenting – but we all know deep down that the only person we can change is ourselves.

Mindfulness challenges us to shift our focus from our partner's faults and explore the ways we can use the tough times to grow. All relationships go through peaks and troughs, particularly when children become part of the equation and there seems to be so much more at stake. At times, we may have the most amazing feeling of being on an incredible, joyful journey together. At others, we may feel that we are carrying a lot on our own. Staying mindful helps us to observe these inevitable cycles without getting too caught up in the gap-filling and story-telling of our 'frenemy' minds. Just as we nurture the HEART-values of Humility, Empathy, Authenticity, Respect and Trust in our relationship with our children, we can also aspire to embody the same values in relation to our partner, however hard this may sometimes be.

Becoming more aware isn't going to transform our relationships overnight, but it can help us to start to see with greater clarity how our partners can trigger strong reactions in us. The people whom we love the most have the greatest power to hurt us, so we can easily react without thinking, particularly when we're feeling stressed, tired or overwhelmed. At times like these, practising mindfulness in relation to our partner – particularly with kids around – can feel practically impossible. A lot of the time it *will* be impossible – and that's okay. The important thing is to keep doing our best to come back to the here and now, and ask ourselves what would be the optimal response in any given moment, rather than getting swept up into the same old routines.

By slowly learning to observe the kinds of thoughts and feelings we are having, we can gradually get better at noticing when we're losing our poise. We can still get angry, or say what we need to say, but we're in control of what we're doing – our feelings are no longer controlling us. We learn to speak our truth clearly and draw appropriate boundaries, and our greater awareness gives us a greater capacity to resist any impulse to lash out or shut down. Above all, we remember to be kind to ourselves and recognize that the challenges of relationships can be our greatest teachers.

Let's take a look at some of the ways you can apply mindfulness in relationships that I find most helpful when working with parents.

Showing appreciation to our partner

In the whirlwind of parenting, it's especially important to make sure that when we do have an opportunity to show our partner we care, we do so in a way that will be most meaningful to them. Although there are endless ways we can show appreciation for each other, all of us have our unique soft spots. For some, hugs or physical affection are all-important. Others will be delighted when their partner cooks a nice meal, takes on a chore or provides some form of practical support with the kids. Even buying a small surprise gift or paying a special compliment can have a big impact – and never underestimate the power of sincere encouragement and praise.

Despite the importance of exchanging these signs of affection, it's very common for one parent to have only a vague idea of the gestures that will be most meaningful to their partner – and to struggle to express their own preferences in return. I've found that it helps parents to reflect on what they most appreciate and share their insights with each other. This can be a simple yet powerful way to nurture greater closeness.

Reading cues

We talked in Session 6 about how a child's acting-up can often be a bid for attention. Just as we can cultivate the ability to see more deeply into what's underlying our child's behaviour, we can also practise paying greater attention to the impact of our everyday interactions with our partner.

According to the clinical psychologist and marriage researcher Dr John Gottman, it's the 'small stuff' in relationships – such as when our partner smiles and gives us a hug or brings us a cup of coffee – that are far more important than people might realize. They may seem insignificant, but these everyday 'bids' for attention are attempts by our partners to establish intimacy.

We all know how easy it is to get so caught up in the pressures of daily life, or even any resentment we may feel towards our partner, that we can take these seemingly small gestures for granted, or fail to notice them at all. Dr Gottman's research suggests that paying attention to the seemingly humdrum interactions that form the everyday fabric of our relationship plays a crucial role in maintaining a vibrant connection.

Watching our own reactions – and choosing a new response

In the same way that we inherit ideas about parenting from the way we were brought up, we also carry templates of how relationships work based on what we experienced in childhood. The way our parents related to each other, or to us, can exert a huge influence on how we communicate with our partner – often without us even knowing. For example, we may see that we're behaving irrationally in our relationships, but we don't know why, or how we might try to change.

A lot of what we are feeling isn't actually about what's happening in the present; it's an echo from the past. As young children, before we developed the ability to use language and think logically, our bodies would store up memories of strong emotions – particularly when we felt angry, scared or ashamed. Conflicts in our intimate relationships can bring these feelings flooding back when they remind us of these early experiences, even if we can't consciously remember them. The stress response in the body can quickly be activated and we can start to feel out of control. Situations in our adult relationships can make us feel as if we're being hijacked and forced to revisit the intense emotions we first felt as helpless children.

We don't need to analyse everything that happened in our childhood to harness the power of mindfulness to help us ride the waves in the here and now. We can remember to take five deep breaths, tune in to the sensations in our bodies and observe the thoughts taking shape in our minds. We don't need to *do* anything – we just need to pause and watch. By observing the reaction as it occurs inside us – rather than immediately acting on it – we break its spell. Whilst we can't change the past, we don't have to let it run our lives in the present.

It is wonderful if your partner can join you on this journey, but even if they would much prefer to throw this book out of the window rather than read it, then you can still choose to take greater responsibility for managing your own reactions. Often, your partner will sense a change in you – and may begin to respond differently in return. Or they might not. Whatever happens, you will be in a far better position to approach your relationship with clarity and make choices that serve you.

Secure, anxious or avoidant: learning about 'attachment styles'

Just as we all learned about relationships by observing our own parents or care-givers, our children will learn from us. If you want to gain greater clarity about the kinds of patterns that might be at work in your relationship with your partner, then I recommend picking up a book exploring 'attachment styles' – common patterns of relating to partners that many of us will recognize. (For some suggestions, see Resources, page 253.) These patterns are usually the result of the kinds of experiences we had growing up. There are three main categories, as explained by Dr Amir Levine and Rachel Heller in their book *Attached*:

- **Secure.** We feel confident in our ability to maintain healthy, long-term relationships and tend to form consistent, stable partnerships.

- **Anxious.** We often find ourselves feeling anxiety over whether our partner truly loves us, and struggle with frequent feelings of insecurity and jealousy.

- **Avoidant.** We fear intimacy and often struggle to commit, or find ourselves pushing partners we love away without knowing why.

While people with secure attachment styles will tend to be drawn together, it's frequently the case that those with anxious attachment styles attract avoidants and vice-versa. This can lead to prolonged dramas in our relationships: cycles of breaking up and getting back together again, or relationships which seem to be forever in crisis but which neither partner seems willing to let go. Such relationships can be very intense, but both sides struggle to meet each other's needs or feel that they really understand one another.

This can cause a great deal of confusion for both partners, and have a big impact on your children, so it's well worth exploring this subject further if you recognize these tendencies in your own relationships. Understanding attachment styles was a huge breakthrough in my own personal journey, and I know many others have benefited just as much from these insights.

Gratitude

As we saw in Session 3, practising gratitude can be one of the most potent ways for us to foster a greater sense of well-being in our daily lives. The same applies in our relationships. When the stresses of raising children are causing tensions with our partner, it's easy to focus on their faults and forget the qualities that drew us to them in the first place. Even when things are going well, we can easily take each other for granted. Here are some questions you might consider if you want to tap into your well of gratitude. Try to come up with three answers for each:

- What do I feel grateful for in my partner?

- What do I appreciate about my partner's relationship with our kids?

- What do I appreciate about myself as a partner?

- What attracted me to my partner in the first place?

- What special moments have we shared in our lives together?

- What can I say or do to show my partner I appreciate them?

It's difficult to feel grateful for someone when we're feeling angry or annoyed – but the more we practise gratitude during calmer moments, the deeper the reserves we'll have to draw on when times are tougher.

Mindful speaking

As we learn to pause and observe our thoughts and physical sensations, so we can also pay greater attention to the words we use. Just as we carefully weigh the impact of what we say on our children, so we can gain a greater awareness of the way our words affect our partner. And we can also ask ourselves whether there are things we need to say that we're holding back, whether it's to do with the kids or something between us. Clear communication takes courage, but it's the only way our relationship will thrive, especially in the context of parenting. It helps to keep some of our attention rooted in our body, particularly when we're broaching difficult issues. This will help to keep us in the here and now, and to speak with greater clarity.

We can bring the same awareness into our interactions with our family and friends, whether in person or online. We all need to offload, and it can be very helpful to seek comfort and advice when we're struggling. But though those close to us may offer advice with the best of intentions, they won't necessarily appreciate the whole picture. Our friends can also start filling in gaps and getting worked up on our behalf. Before you know it, you've created a whole story together about what's going on in your partner's head that may be a complete work of fiction. Our friends can be wonderful listeners, but let's be discerning about the advice we take on board. The most important person you can talk to about your relationship is your partner.

Mindful listening

We saw in Session 6 how the practice of paying more attention as you listen to your child can deepen a HEART-centred connection. We can use the same kind of deliberate attentiveness to strengthen our bond with our partner. We can bring particular attention to the way we give praise – to both our partners and our children (see box below). No matter where we are in life, we all long to be validated and heard.

If we find we're having trouble listening, it may be that our own feelings are taking over. We may need to offload through a good chat with a friend before we will feel light enough to provide a compassionate ear for our partner. With the pressures of childcare, it can be difficult to find space for an uninterrupted conversation, but taking time to be fully present can strengthen your foundations as a family. I've seen mums and dads rescue their relationships from the rockiest of patches by making time to truly listen to each other.

Praising Your Partner

As the psychologist Dr Martin Seligman argues in his book *Flourish*, praise tends to have the greatest positive impact when we take a moment to help somebody relive and explore the reasons why something good happened to them. This does not necessarily come naturally, but it can have very powerful results. Ask them to walk you through precisely how they heard the good news, what they think they had done to deserve it and how it made them feel.

For example, let's assume your partner has taken your child out for a special day-trip as a treat. You could ask them to describe exactly how the day unfolded and recall the various ways in which your child responded. Ask them how they came up with the idea and why they think your child enjoyed it so much. Do something to show your appreciation – even something relatively simple like buying a cake or a bottle of wine. The more interest you show and the more questions you ask, the longer your partner will be able to dwell in the warm glow of their accomplishment.

Making time

Given that parenting is all about building a family unit, it's poignant to acknowledge how lonely it can often feel. Finding ways to spend time together as partners – rather than purely in our role as parents – can help us remember why we got together in the first place, and cement our feeling of being in a team, rather than two individuals waging separate battles. It's not selfish to create an opportunity to have a chat about what you're both feeling and how you can best support each other. Taking a break from your kids – however difficult it may be – to deepen your appreciation for one another is an act of love for all the family.

Handling conflict

If we ever share our holiday pictures on social media, then the chances are that we choose images of our family smiling and laughing on the beach or in a restaurant. Few of us post pictures documenting the other side of family life: siblings bickering, kids throwing tantrums and parents shouting at each other. We generally try to keep our arguments behind closed doors, but the reality is that friction is an inevitable part of family life and nothing to feel ashamed about. The picture-perfect family ideal is a myth.

Just like our children, our partners have an unerring ability to know how to poke us in our weak spots, or say or do the very thing that's guaranteed to tip us over the edge. Such behaviour can often feel as though it's deliberately designed to antagonize us – though sometimes, if we're able to step back, we can see that our partners are struggling just as much as we are. Here are some of the most common sources of tension between parents I encounter in my work:

- **Not feeling appreciated.** Mums or dads who do not go to work can start to miss the kind of professional validation that goes with having a job outside the home. Partners who do work may in turn struggle to strike a balance between the demands of their job and their family. Neither is getting the recognition or support they need.

● **Feeling criticized.** Criticism from our partner can easily trigger the feelings of anger or shame we felt as children when we were told off by our parents – which is why harsh words can hurt so much and make us feel vulnerable.

● **Clashing parenting styles.** Different ideas about discipline or how to handle a child in distress can become a chronic source of friction. Both parents can feel criticized, judged or disrespected, and the gulf widens further.

● **Lack of intimacy.** A lack of physical intimacy can weaken a relationship and lead to feelings of frustration and jealousy. Making time for each other, however difficult, is important.

● **Not having enough.** Whether it's time, money, energy, holidays, space or affection – many couples feel a sense of 'lack' in some form that can strain their relationship to breaking point.

If there's a single thread that runs through almost all the stories I hear in my work, it's the difficulty parents have in forgiving themselves for losing their temper with their partner in front of the kids. We find it hard to accept that conflict is not something to feel guilty over: arguments can clear the path to resolving issues and allow us fully to express how we feel. The most important thing is not to avoid or suppress conflicts, but learn how to work through the difficult feelings that they bring to the surface. Mindfulness can help us to remain centred even when confronting the toughest of times. By demonstrating that we're trying to work things out, we model a valuable skill for our children.

When conflict arises, we will have a much better chance of handling it effectively if we can remain as present as possible, while remembering to be kind to ourselves, particularly when we're feeling hurt. It can take time to rebuild, especially if there has been a breach of trust. The simplest tools for repairing our bond are among the most powerful:

- **Mindful pause.** Before you react, take a pause – and five deep breaths. Is this the moment to confront an issue? Or would it be better to address it when you are both feeling calmer? Letting even a few minutes pass can soften the mood and give you time to reflect and consider your response.

- **Connect with compassion.** Is it possible to feel compassion for your partner? It may be easier to forgive when you begin to realize that they have also been struggling with hurt feelings or resentments in the same way you have. For example, you may feel that your partner is not offering you enough emotional support, especially when the kids are playing up. Equally, your partner may feel that they're trying their best to help you but that you don't appreciate their efforts. By sharing these difficult feelings without blaming each other, both parents can start to find ways to support each other more effectively.

- **Be fully there.** Being fully present and listening mindfully to what our partner is saying – rather than jumping in – can give them the gift of being fully heard and create a space for something new to enter. And as we have seen earlier, celebrating achievements, big or small, can be a powerful demonstration of our appreciation and strengthen our connection.

- **Taking responsibility.** However much we may want to point the finger at our partner and prove that we're in the right, it can be far more constructive to focus on explaining how we are feeling rather than dwelling on what they have or haven't done. Instead of using 'blame statements' that may put our partner on the defensive, we can use 'I am' statements that reveal our vulnerability. For example, instead of saying, 'You never bother to let me know when you're going to be late home from work,' you might say, 'I am feeling really upset because I don't feel like you care enough about me to let me know when you're going to be late.'

● **Kindness.** Treating ourselves as kindly as possible when we are navigating relationships is one of the best things we can do for ourselves and our families – all the time remembering that conflict and arguments are something we all experience.

There are also steps you can take during the more harmonious periods in a relationship to ensure that any conflicts that do arise serve a useful purpose by airing important issues and bringing underlying conflicts into the open. Here are some ideas:

● **Time out.** Agree in advance with your partner that you will step back if there's a flare-up to take a few moments to centre yourselves. It can help to agree a specific form of words, such as, 'I'm going to take a pause now.' As you make this agreement, you can both acknowledge that this time out is not a sign of rejection or an attempt to avoid an issue.

● **Identifying triggers.** It can help to figure out the specific kinds of situations that tend to cause tension. Possibilities could include:

- Feeling criticized
- Feeling taken for granted
- Jealousy
- Feeling a partner is not pulling their weight
- Criticism of those you care about (family/friends)
- Being rejected in a bid for physical affection
- Feeling ignored

Once you've identified these triggers, talk about them with your partner. You will feel better for being heard and they will understand you more and be better placed to avoid inadvertently upsetting you.

- **Ground rules.** It can work well to set aside certain times to discuss thorny issues – and it is a good idea to avoid particularly stressful times, such as the end of the work day or late at night. Agreeing to discuss things at a moment that works for both of you will make things much easier.

Rather than seeing conflicts as signs of failure, we can use them as valuable opportunities to learn about each other and ourselves. By showing our children that it's possible to repair breaches, you can teach them that arguments can occur between people who love each other and that they can be reconciled. Conflict can then be harnessed as an opportunity to deepen our relationship and provide a healthy model for resolving disputes that will serve our children well when they have families of their own.

Sarah: 'We see parenting differently'

'My husband Rob is always so logical and problem-solvy – and I can see that his approach isn't working with our daughter. She is seven and has been diagnosed with ADHD. My husband and I have struggled with her. She's very sensitive to her environment – particularly noise and temperature. My husband kept telling me to turn up the discipline. But she doesn't process information in the same way as we do. She got scared by being shouted at. Everything at school and home was impacting on her self-esteem. I ended up trying to protect my daughter from her dad.

'I told Rob, "You need to approach her more gently than our other children." They're more robust, but she gets so scared by being shouted at.

'My husband didn't understand. He just thought she was being naughty. Once she had a medical diagnosis, he backed off a bit as he realized that there was a reason why she was different to other children. He understands now, but he's still too hard. She's scared of him.

Continued ...

'Of course she needs limits – but harsh discipline doesn't work with her. She needs empathy, validation – to be heard and listened to so she can calm down. Then he can do the problem-solving when she is in a much more receptive place.

'We've often clashed because of our different approaches. Rob will crack down on something the kids have done, while I will be more laid back, and say that he doesn't understand the context. Like when it comes to bedtime – I've never looked too closely at the clock, I just see how the day pans out. Rob is more structured. He would prefer to know that 8 p.m. is bedtime. But sometimes the kids might not be ready to go to bed, or they're not in the mood for a story.

'Home doesn't feel very harmonious right now. It's very stressful and I know kids pick up on the bad vibes between parents. I just wish he would be a bit more tuned in to them and understand that the children's emotional needs are important too. They aren't deliberately being naughty, but they haven't yet learned to manage their big feelings.'

Saying goodbye

Everyone wants to experience a deep sense of connection with their partners, but it doesn't always turn out that way. So many of us can feel a nagging doubt that our relationships could be so much better, and we can experience a great deal of frustration and sadness when we feel this hoped-for harmony is just out of reach. We may find it difficult to be truly honest about how we're feeling because we're scared of the changes the truth may bring.

Sometimes we're not consciously aware there is a problem and simply resign ourselves to the conflicts and arguments, the snappiness, the irritable comments or the silent treatment. We may spend years wrestling with a dilemma: should we separate, or would it be better for our kids if we grit our teeth and stay together? There may come a point when our differences are so great that we feel as if we're hitting our head against a brick wall and we may conclude – after a lot of heartache and soul-searching – that our only option is to move on.

Even when we're certain we're making the right decision, the end of any relationship can bring up profound feelings of guilt, failure, bitterness or shame. Or we may not have a choice because our partner has ended our relationship – perhaps by having an affair or simply by walking away. The sad reality is that not all conflicts can be solved, and not all relationships are destined to last. One thing is for certain: in the aftermath of a break-up, compassion for ourselves becomes more important than ever.

When facing the kinds of intense emotions that can accompany an ending, it can be difficult to find the time and space you need to recover from the shock and surround yourself with the friends and family who can help you through. When it feels as if all the life force has been sucked out of you, it can be hard enough just to stay on top of the demands of childcare, work and other responsibilities, let alone devote energy to being kind to yourself and coming to terms with what's happened. Everything's about pushing through and surviving.

In all this turmoil, it's often hard to think straight. It's obviously important to find an age-appropriate way to explain what's happening to your child – and above all to reinforce the message that the end of the relationship is not their fault. As we all know, children are sponges – even the youngest ones pick up more information than we may assume – but they don't have the full picture. Perhaps even more than adults, children are prone to filling in gaps. It's common for them to blame themselves for their parents' difficulties, and it's vital to find a way to make sure they understand that they are not the cause of your adult problems.

It's also important to consider carefully what you say about your ex and any new partner they may meet, and resist any temptation to speak badly of them in front of your child. If you need to vent, speak to friends or family. This may be easier said than done – particularly if any kind of abuse has taken place. If you are struggling, it's okay to tell your child you are finding things difficult, all the while stressing that they are not to blame.

I have worked with a number of parents who have felt a great deal of remorse about over-sharing their relationship struggles, realizing that their children have taken on too much of their emotional burden. Parents in this situation often say things like, 'My child shouldn't know this much. I want him to enjoy being a child, not feel responsible for our relationship.' If you feel this might have happened, it's worth acknowledging it to your child. Children have a remarkable capacity to forgive when they sense an apology is sincere. This can be an opportunity to role-model authenticity and accept the fact that everyone makes mistakes and that all of us are only human.

Single parents

Being a single parent brings its own challenges. Some of us choose to go it alone and are very happy to raise our children in a single-parent family. For others, living outside the 'conventional' set-up can generate mixed feelings. There may be anger or grief over what 'might have been', or even a sense of shame for not having been able to make our relationship work. We may harbour feelings of guilt for what our child witnessed during a break-up or divorce. Taking time out to care for yourself may be that much harder, and it's not always easy to be both a mum and a dad rolled into one. It may be hard to look around at friends who are in couples – particularly when your children are playing up, or you are feeling overwhelmed with responsibilities and you could do with some back-up. Managing the relationship with an ex-partner and the need to agree on access to children can be a source of yet more friction and uncertainty.

However you may feel about your ex, it's preferable – if at all possible – to work together as a team as far as you can for the sake of your child. Obviously, if you have major disagreements and differences in your approach to parenting, this can be a real challenge. However, it might still be possible at least to attempt to smooth the transitions between your households by sharing information on the routines your child is used to, what they eat and so on. A child can find it confusing when parents have very different schedules – for example, one may have a fixed bedtime, while another may be more flexible. It goes without saying that the more you can set aside your differences and agree on a consistent approach, the better. It's also helpful to give children as much advance warning as possible about when they can expect to be spending time with your ex so that the transition feels less abrupt. The situation may never be ideal, but this doesn't mean that you can't use every opportunity you find to strengthen a HEART-centred connection with your child.

The arrival of a new partner in a single-parent household will herald more changes. While some children love having a new parental figure in their home, others can feel neglected or jealous because they've got so used to having you to themselves. It's important to communicate with your child clearly, validate their feelings and make a point of carving out special time for them so they are less likely to feel neglected. Here are some tips I share with single parents on this path:

- **Talk.** Give a child ample opportunity to discuss how they feel and encourage them to express themselves honestly, openly and without judgement. You may not like all they tell you, but at least you have created a safe space where they are able to talk candidly with you.

- **Validate.** Validate any feelings the new situation may trigger in the child, from fear and anxiety to anger and jealousy. Show that you understand how they are feeling and that there's nothing wrong with their reaction.

- **No such thing as 'normal'.** Allow yourself to acknowledge that each family is different, and there is no shame attached to deviating from 'conventional' norms.

It can also be a great help to discuss values your 'inner parent' holds dear with your new partner to explore the common ground you share, and to work together to find ways to express these values in your approach to raising your children.

*

The five key points

Parenting as a team

- Relationships change when children arrive: feeling supported is key.

- Making time to reconnect is a gift for yourself, your partner and your children.

- Pay attention to the everyday: appreciation and gratitude make a big difference.

- Children 'fill in gaps' too: find ways to talk if there's a conflict.

- Parenting styles may differ, but we can agree to work as a team.

Afterword

Being a parent is hard. We aspire to do the best we can in every moment, but there will be times when we feel disappointment, a sense of failure or regret. These feelings are inevitable. Indeed, we are all conditioned to respond to challenges in the present by what happened in our past. We may make a sincere effort to change, only to discover that our habitual ways of thinking and behaving have enormous momentum. Slipping once again into an old pattern of self-blame, we can lose hope that we'll ever be able to approach life differently. This is true of every human being. The struggles we face as individuals are merely aspects of a collective, planetary predicament reflected in the many crises facing humanity as a whole.

My goal in writing this book was to invite you to consider a simple proposition: you are more powerful than you think. We don't need to perfect the art of mindfulness to make an impact in our own lives – and the lives of others. Each time we manage to step back for a moment from our 'frenemy' mind counts for more than we might assume. Each time we manage to show ourselves and others a little more kindness and compassion, we send a positive ripple through the living web that connects us all. Each time we can take a moment to truly listen strengthens our HEART-centred connection with our daughter, son, or partner. Every child who feels supported, nurtured and understood – and every parent who feels a little more confident – is like another bulb lighting up.

If you have read this far then the chances are that you have already begun to sense the kind of shift in perspective that mindfulness can offer. As we start to practise in whatever way feels right for us, we begin to see the effects accumulate over time. It's as if a new dimension has opened in our lives – one where we have more choice over how we think and feel than we had imagined possible. Some of the exercises or stories in this book may speak to you more directly than others, but I emphasize that *Five Deep Breaths* is intended merely as a gateway, and I encourage you to explore further for yourself. There are some suggestions for books, groups and organizations I have found helpful on my own journeys with parents in the following pages, but there is no set path. Give yourself permission to make a little time to read more widely in this field or try a new workshop or course. Or simply reach out to others. Share your experiences, and understand that you are not alone in your struggle for greater balance and harmony. These are simple steps but you may be surprised at where they lead.

A great deal is written these days in the media about the mental health 'crisis' gripping our current generation of teens – and the growing numbers of children also seeking help. There is no doubt that this should be a source of grave concern for everybody who cares about the future of this country. But there is another side to this story. Every day in my work with children and teenagers, I am struck by how much more willing they are to open up and explore their thoughts and feelings than I was at their age. The courage shown by so many young people in seeking to confront and resolve their difficult emotions – rather than suppress or numb them – should be an inspiration to us all. While doing our best to support our sons and daughters, we should always remember that they have much to teach.

Nevertheless, the real sense of distress and being overwhelmed that so many families are experiencing is a clear sign that things need to change. Just as life has a habit of giving us the sometimes challenging lessons we need to learn as individuals to develop our highest potential, so it seems our society has arrived at a point where we need fundamentally to rethink the system we use to educate our children and mitigate some of the unnecessary stress it causes to pupils, parents and teachers. I have no doubt that there is an archetypal 'inner parent' watching over our country – and she is willing us to begin this endeavour as a matter of urgency. As individuals, it's easy to feel powerless, but let's not forget that every one of our thoughts, words and deeds reverberates in space and time in ways we can never fully perceive. Every kind act, every deep breath and every mindful pause counts.

If this book can encourage a few mums and dads to trust their intuition a little more often and go a bit easier on themselves then it will have fulfilled its purpose. But my sincere hope is that as these small steps multiply, their impact will spread beyond individual families and gradually foster the kinds of changes we need to see in society as a whole, and in particular in our classrooms. As more of us place our faith in our 'inner parent', the more chance we'll have of coming together to create schools that place as much emphasis on cultivating resilience, creativity and compassion as they do on exam results, and where emotional intelligence, love of nature and well-being are prized as much as academic excellence. We'll need to listen to our hearts as well as our heads if we're going to succeed in the most important task facing Britain today: raising a generation of happier, healthier kids who aren't programmed to conform, but who are brimming with enthusiasm for building a society fit for all our futures.

References

Session 1

page 19 Vagus nerve: Bergland, Christopher, 'The neurobiology of grace under pressure', *Psychology Today*, 2 February 2013

page 19 Bergland, Christopher, 'How does the vagus nerve convey gut instincts to the brain?', *Psychology Today*, 23 May 2014

page 19 Cuda, Gretchen, 'Just breathe: Body has a built-in stress reliever', *NPR*, 6 December 2010

Session 2

page 24 Parliamentary Report on Mindfulness: Mindfulness All-Party Parliamentary Group (MAPPG), *Mindful Nation UK*, October 2015

page 25 Being versus doing: Kabat-Zinn, Jon, *Wherever You Go, There You Are: Mindfulness Meditation for Everyday Life*, London: Piatkus Books, 2004

page 30 Observer mind: Tolle, Eckhart, *The Power of Now: A Guide to Spiritual Enlightenment*, London: Yellow Kite, 2001

page 30 Thinking traps: Beck, Aaron, *Depression: Clinical, Experimental, and Theoretical Aspects*, New York: Harper & Row, 1967

—— Burns, David, *The Feeling Good Handbook*, New York: William Morrow and Company, 1989

page 39 Labelling thoughts: Harris, Russ, *The Happiness Trap (Based on ACT: A Revolutionary Mindfulness-based Programme for Overcoming Stress, Anxiety and Depression)*, London: Robinson, 2008

page 39 Co-founders of Acceptance and Commitment Therapy: Hayes, Steven, Strosahl, Kirk, and Wilson, Kelly, *Acceptance and Commitment*

Therapy: An Experiential Approach to Behavior Change, New York: Guildford Press, 1999

Session 3

page 48 Research Center for Healthy Minds: Davidson, Richard, www.centerhealthyminds.org/about/overview

page 61 Brain-imaging study on meditation: Lutz, Antoine, et al., 'Long-term meditators self-induce high-amplitude gamma synchrony during mental practice', *Proceedings of the National Academy of Sciences*, 2004

page 63 Children's kindness project: Action for Happiness, 'Children's kindness project inspires commuters', www.actionforhappiness.org/news/childrens-kindness-project-inspires-commuters, 28 November 2014

page 64 Acts of kindness: Russell, Bernadette, *Do Nice, Be Kind, Spread Happy: Acts of Kindness for Kids (Random Acts of Kindness)*, Brighton: Ivy Press, 2014

page 64 Hooper, Ryan, and Heads, Laura, '"I wanted to cry": Young mum receives heartwarming letter from stranger on train', *Mirror*, 25 January 2015

page 64 Beattie, Kieran, 'Kind-hearted Aberdeen schoolboy, 7, donates birthday presents to local food bank', *Press and Journal*, 1 February 2016

page 64 Moran, Lee, 'Store worker's beautiful deed for blind girl with autism goes viral', *Huffington Post*, 8 May 2016

Session 4

page 80 Comprehensive Resource Model of therapy breathing techniques – CRM Ocean Breathing, CRM Earth Breathing and CRM Heart Breathing: Schwarz, Lisa, et al., *The Comprehensive Resource Model: Effective Therapeutic Techniques for the Healing of Complex Trauma (Explorations in Mental Health)*, London: Routledge, 2016

Session 5

page 87 History of parenting: Watson, John, *Psychological Care of Infant and Child*, New York: W. W. Norton, 1928

—— Spock, Benjamin, *The Common Sense Book of Baby and Child Care*, New York: Duell, Sloan and Pearce, 1946

page 88 Origins of attachment research: Bowlby, John, 'The Nature of the Child's Tie to His Mother', *International Journal of Psycho-Analysis*, 1958

—— Bowlby, John, 'Separation Anxiety', *International Journal of Psycho-Analysis*, 1959

page 91 HeartMath Institute in California: www.heartmath.com

page 106 Building resilience: Neufeld, Gordon, and Maté, Gabor, *Hold on to Your Kids: Why Parents Need to Matter More Than Peers*, New York: Ballantine Books, 2006

page 108 Growth mindset: Dweck, Carol, *Mindset: How You Can Fulfil Your Potential*, London: Robinson, 2012

Session 6

page 120 Active listening: Rogers, Carl, and Evans Farson, Richard, *Active Listening*, Chicago: University of Chicago Industrial Relations Center, 1957

page 125 Power animals: Schwarz, Lisa, et al., *The Comprehensive Resource Model: Effective Therapeutic Techniques for the Healing of Complex Trauma (Explorations in Mental Health)*, London: Routledge, 2016

page 130 Report about referrals to the Tavistock Gender Identity Development Service: Lyons, Kate, 'Gender identity clinic services under strain as referral rates soar', *Guardian*, 10 July 2016

page 133 Dry-eyed syndrome: Stiffelman, Susan, *Parenting Without Power Struggles: Raising Joyful, Resilient Kids While Staying Cool, Calm, and Connected*, New York: Morgan James Publishing, 2009

REFERENCES

Session 7

page 140 'Upstairs' and 'downstairs' brain/'flipping your lid': Siegel, Daniel, and Payne Bryson, Tina, *The Whole-Brain Child: 12 Revolutionary Strategies to Nurture Your Child's Developing Mind*, New York: Random House Publishing Group, 2011

page 141 'Neural wi-fi': Goleman, Daniel, *Social Intelligence: The New Science of Human Relationships*, New York: Arrow, 2007

page 145 Tend and befriend: Taylor, Shelley, et al., 'Biobehavioral Responses to Stress in Females: Tend-and-Befriend, not Fight-or-Flight', *Psychological Review*, 2000

page 153 Glitter jar: Willard, Christopher, *Growing Up Mindful: Essential Practices to Help Children, Teens, and Families Find Balance, Calm, and Resilience*, Louisville, CO: Sounds True, 2016

page 156 Sensitive children: Aron, Elaine, *The Highly Sensitive Child: Helping Our Children Thrive When the World Overwhelms Them*, New York: Harmony Books, 2002

page 157 'Orchid' and 'dandelion' children: Boyce, Thomas, and Ellis, Bruce, 'Biological Sensitivity to Context', *Development and Psychopathology*, 2005

Session 8

page 166 Wired for risk: Galván, Adriana, 'Why the brains of teenagers excel at taking risks', *Aeon*, 14 June 2016

page 166 Teenage brain: E.B., 'How teenage brains are different', *The Economist*, 18 March 2015

page 166 Disregard for consequences: Siegel, Daniel, *Brainstorm: The Power and Purpose of the Teenage Brain*, New York: Jeremy P. Tarcher/Penguin, 2013

page 167 Sensitivity to peer pressure: Blakemore, Sarah-Jayne, *The Mysterious Workings of the Adolescent Brain*, TEDGlobal, 2012

page 167 Interpretation of facial expression: van Beek, Yolanda, and Semon Dubas, Judith, 'Age and gender differences in decoding basic and non-basic facial expressions in late childhood and early adolescence', *Journal of Nonverbal Behavior*, 2008

——Yurgelun-Todd, Deborah, 'Emotional and cognitive changes during adolescence', *Current Opinion in Neurobiology*, 2007

page 168 Out of sync: Foster, Russell, 'Why teenagers really do need an extra hour in bed', *New Scientist*, 17 April 2013

page 168 Teensleep project at University of Oxford:
www.ndcn.ox.ac.uk/research/sleep-circadian-neuroscience-institute/research-projects-4/teensleep

page 176 'Name it to tame it': Siegel, Daniel, and Payne Bryson, Tina, *The Whole-Brain Child: 12 Revolutionary Strategies to Nurture Your Child's Developing Mind*, New York: Random House Publishing Group, 2011

page 188 Role of mentors: Biddulph, Steve, *Raising Boys: Why Boys Are Different – and How to Help Them Become Happy and Well-Balanced Men*, Warriewood, NSW: Finch Publishing, 1997

Session 9

page 190 The term 'Digital Natives' was coined by the US writer and speaker on education Marc Prensky in 2001: Prensky, Marc, 'Digital Natives, Digital Immigrants', *On the Horizon*, Bradford: MCB University Press, 2001

page 195 BeatYourselfUpBook: Keegan, Natalie, 'Mumsnet user calls for mums not to compare themselves to others on "BeatYourself Up Book"', *Sun*, 3 April 2016

Session 10

page 213 Reading cues in relationships: Gottman, John, *The Relationship Cure: A 5 Step Guide for Building Better Connections with Family, Friends and Lovers*, New York: Crown Publications, 2001

page 215 Attachment styles: Levine, Amir, and Heller, Rachel, *Attached: Identify Your Attachment Style and Find Your Perfect Match*, New York: Penguin, 2010

page 218 Praising your partner: Seligman, Martin, *Flourish: A Visionary New Understanding of Happiness and Well-being*, New York: Atria, 2012

Resources

Mental health support organizations for adults

Mental Health Foundation

www.mentalhealth.org.uk

A mental health research, policy and service-improvement charity that aims to improve the lives of those with mental health problems or learning disabilities.

Mind

www.mind.org.uk

A charity providing mental health advice and support. Mind also campaigns to improve services, raise awareness and promote understanding.

No Panic

www.nopanic.org.uk

Helpline: 0844 967 4848

Voluntary charity offering support for sufferers of panic attacks and Obsessive Compulsive Disorder (OCD).

Relate: The Relationship People

www.relate.org.uk

Helpline: 0300 100 1234

Every year Relate helps more than a million people of all ages, backgrounds and sexual orientations to strengthen their relationships through its counselling services.

Samaritans

www.samaritans.org

Helpline: 116 123

Samaritans is available 24 hours a day to provide confidential emotional support to people experiencing feelings of distress, despair or suicidal thoughts.

Finding a therapist

Association for Family Therapy and Systemic Practice (AFT)

www.aft.org.uk

Britain's leading organization for family therapy and systemic psychotherapists. Its members work with children, young people and adults, couples, families and individuals.

British Association for Counselling and Psychotherapy (BACP)

www.bacp.co.uk

A professional body for counsellors and psychotherapists accredited by the Professional Standards Authority for Health and Social Care.

British Psychological Society (BPS)

www.bps.org.uk

The British Psychological Society is the representative body for psychology and psychologists in Britain, and is responsible for the development, promotion and application of psychology for the public good. Its directory of Chartered Psychologists can help you find a qualified therapist.

Counselling Directory

www.counselling-directory.org.uk

Counselling Directory has developed a service that brings together all the information needed to help connect people with the right counsellor or professional support for them.

Mindfulness

Be Mindful

www.bemindful.co.uk

Run by the Mental Health Foundation, this programme helps you to learn mindfulness online or find a teacher or course in your area. Courses are nationwide and are secular and science-based.

Mindful

www.mindful.org

A website with lots of information and practical tips from the team behind *Mindful* magazine.

UK Network for Mindfulness-Based Teacher Training Organizations

www.mindfulness-network.org/listingspagenew.php

A directory of mindfulness teachers who have demonstrated that they meet UK good practice guidelines. It includes lists of affiliated organizations and resources.

Meditation Centres

Gaia House

www.gaiahouse.co.uk

Gaia House is a meditation retreat centre offering silent meditation retreats in the Buddhist tradition.

London Insight Meditation

www.londoninsight.org

This small, independent charity promotes insight meditation, plus related practices, values and teachings from the Buddhist tradition.

Vipassana Meditation

www.dipa.dhamma.org

This organization offers ten-day residential silent retreats to learn Vipassana meditation. Courses are run on a donation-only basis.

Organizations for young people and parents

Action for Children

www.actionforchildren.org.uk

A charity committed to helping vulnerable and neglected children and young people.

Childline

www.childline.org.uk

Helpline: 0800 1111

Childline is a private and confidential service for children and young people up to the age of nineteen. Call their helpline, chat online, or send an email.

Family Lives

www.familylives.org.uk

Helpline: 0808 800 2222

A national family-support charity providing parenting help and support in all aspects of family life.

MindEd

www.minded.org.uk

Parents who are concerned about their child's mental health and well-being can visit this excellent site to access good-quality information. MindEd also features advice from parents who support children with mental health problems.

Mindfulness in Schools Project (MiSP)

www.mindfulnessinschools.org

MiSP was established in 2009 as a not-for-profit organization. It aims to bring mindfulness to young people and those who care for them in order to advance their well-being and resilience.

National Children's Bureau

www.ncb.org.uk

A charitable organization dedicated to advancing the health and well-being of all children and young people across every aspect of their lives, and providing them with a powerful and authoritative voice.

NSPCC

www.nspcc.org.uk

Helpline: 0808 800 5000

A leading charity aiming to prevent child abuse and help children and families recover from its effects. If you're worried about a child – even if you're unsure – you can contact their professional counsellors 24 hours a day for help, advice and support.

Papyrus

www.papyrus-uk.org

Helpline: 0800 068 4141

A national charity dedicated to the prevention of young suicide, Papyrus runs a confidential helpline called HOPELineUK for young persons at risk of suicide and anybody who is worried about them.

Reading Well Books on Prescription

www.reading-well.org.uk

A source of recommendations for expert-endorsed books about mental health aimed at thirteen- to eighteen-year-olds. It covers topics including anxiety, stress and OCD, as well as bullying and exams. Books are available to borrow from public libraries.

YoungMinds
www.youngminds.org.uk

Helpline for parents: 0808 802 5544

A charity committed to improving the emotional well-being and mental health of children and young people. Provides information for parents and professionals, runs training workshops, campaigns and conducts research.

Further reading and helpful organizations for specific issues

Anxiety and anger

Collins-Donnelly, Kate, *Starving the Anxiety Gremlin: A Cognitive Behavioural Therapy Workbook on Anxiety Management for Young People*, Gremlin and Thief CBT Workbook, London: Jessica Kingsley Publishers, 2013

Creswell, Cathy, and Willetts, Lucy, *Overcoming Your Child's Fears and Worries: A Self-help Guide Using Cognitive Behavioral Techniques*, London: Robinson, 2007

Huebner, Dawn, *What to Do When You Worry Too Much: A Kid's Guide to Overcoming Anxiety (What to Do Guides for Kids)*, Washington, DC: Magination Press, 2005

Siegel, Daniel, and Payne Bryson, Tina, *The Whole-Brain Child: 12 Revolutionary Strategies to Nurture Your Child's Developing Mind*, New York: Random House Publishing Group, 2011

Whitehouse, Éliane, and Pudney, Warwick, *A Volcano in My Tummy: Helping Children to Handle Anger*, Gabriola, BC: New Society Publishers, 1998

Autism Spectrum Disorder (ASD)

National Autistic Society (NAS)

www.autism.org.uk

Helpline: 0808 800 4104

Provides information for parents and carers about autism and runs an online community and a confidential parent-to-parent telephone service.

Bereavement

Winston's Wish: The Charity for Bereaved Children

www.winstonswish.org.uk

Helpline: 08088 020 021

Support, guidance and information for anyone caring for a bereaved child or a child facing the imminent death of a family member.

Child Bereavement UK

www.childbereavementuk.org

Helpline: 0800 02 888 40

Supports families and educates professionals when a baby or child of any age dies or is dying, or when a child is facing bereavement.

Cruse Bereavement Care

www.cruse.org.uk

Helpline: 0808 808 1677

Promotes the well-being of bereaved people and aims to enable anyone who has been bereaved to understand their grief and cope with their loss.

Body image

Be Real Campaign
www.berealcampaign.co.uk

A national movement of individuals, schools, businesses, charities and public bodies campaigning to change attitudes to body image. It was launched in response to the 'Reflections on Body Image' report by the All-Party Parliamentary Group for Body Image.

Body Gossip
www.bodygossip.org

A charity promoting body confidence. It delivers an education programme to teenagers aged 13–18 in secondary schools all over Britain.

Bullying

Bullying UK (Part of Family Lives)
www.bullying.co.uk

Helpline: 0808 800 2222

Offers extensive practical advice and information about bullying for young people, and its website has a section on bullying at school.

Bullybusters
www.bullybusters.org.uk

Helpline: 0800 169 6928

Provides information on bullying and runs an anti-bullying initiative that offers training and awareness sessions for schools, professionals and parents.

Kidscape
www.kidscape.org.uk

Helpline for concerned family members: 0207 823 5430

A charity that equips young people, parents and professionals with the skills to tackle bullying and safeguarding issues across Britain.

Digital technology and online safety

Hayman, Suzie, and Coleman, John, *Parents and Digital Technology: How to Raise the Connected Generation*, London: Routledge, 2016

Janis-Norton, Noel, *Calmer Easier Happier Screen Time: For Parents of Toddlers to Teens, a Guide to Getting Back in Charge of Technology*, London: Yellow Kite, 2016

Childnet
www.childnet.com

A non-profit organization working to help make the internet a great and safe place for children. Includes advice on making family contracts to manage use of the internet.

Cybersmile Foundation
www.cybersmile.org

A non-profit organization tackling all forms of online bullying and hate campaigns.

Internet Matters
www.internetmatters.org

A website that helps parents keep their children safe online. It includes age-specific practical tips and resources covering areas including: parental controls, managing cyberbullying, sexting, inappropriate content and online grooming.

NSPCC and O2
www.nspcc.org.uk and www.o2.co.uk/help/nspcc

Helpline: 0808 800 5002

Phone company O2 has joined forces with the NSPCC to help keep children safe online. Whether you want to set up parental controls, adjust privacy settings or get advice on social networks, you can call experts from O2 and NSPCC on their helpline seven days a week.

Thinkuknow
www.thinkuknow.co.uk

An education programme about sexual abuse underpinned by the latest intelligence from the National Crime Agency's Child Exploitation and Online Protection Centre command. Thinkuknow aims to ensure that children, young people, their parents and carers, and the professionals who work with them, all have access to timely and practical information.

UK Safer Internet Centre
www.saferinternet.org.uk

Helpline: 0344 381 4772

Provides e-safety tips, advice and resources to help children and young people stay safe online.

Drugs and alcohol

Talk to Frank
www.talktofrank.com

Helpline: 0300 123 6600

Confidential helpline and detailed information about drugs and alcohol for families.

Eating disorders

Bryant-Waugh, Rachel, *Eating Disorders: A Parents' Guide*, London: Routledge, 2004

Anorexia and Bulimia Care

www.anorexiabulimiacare.org.uk

Helpline: 03000 11 12 13

A national organization providing care, emotional support and practical guidance for anyone affected by eating disorders: sufferers, their families, carers and professionals.

Beat

www.b-eat.co.uk

Helpline: 0345 634 1414

A charity supporting people affected by eating disorders.

Gender issues

Gender Identity Development Service (GIDS)

www.gids.nhs.uk

Established in 1989, GIDS is a specialized clinic commissioned by NHS England for young people presenting with difficulties with their gender identity.

Obsessive Compulsive Disorder (OCD)

Derisley, Jo, *Breaking Free from OCD: A CBT Guide for Young People and Their Families*, London: Jessica Kingsley Publishers, 2008

OCD-UK

www.ocduk.org

Supporting children and adults affected by OCD.

Play, nature and resilience

Brown, Stuart, and Vaughan, Christopher, *Play: How It Shapes the Brain, Opens the Imagination, and Invigorates the Soul*, New York: Avery/ Putnam, 2009

Ginsburg, Kenneth, *Building Resilience in Children and Teens: Giving Kids Roots and Wings*, Elk Grove Village, IL: American Academy of Pediatrics, 2011

Hanscom, Angela, *Balanced and Barefoot: How Unrestricted Outdoor Play Makes for Strong, Confident, and Capable Children*, Oakland, CA: New Harbinger, 2016

Louv, Richard, *Last Child in the Woods: Saving Our Children from Nature-Deficit Disorder*, London: Atlantic Books, 2010

Self-harm

Smith, Jane, *The Parent's Guide to Self Harm: What Parents Need to Know*, Oxford: Lion Books, 2012

National Self-Harm Network
www.nshn.co.uk

Helpline: 0800 622 6000

A national charity to provide support to people who self-harm, and those affected by self-harm, including family and professionals. They have useful resources that can be downloaded on understanding more about self-harm and strategies to encourage other ways of coping with difficult emotions.

Inspiring organizations for parents and children

Action for Happiness

www.actionforhappiness.org

Members take action in their homes, workplaces, schools and local communities to create a happier world, with fewer people suffering from mental health problems and more people feeling good, functioning well and helping others.

EarthCraftuk

www.earthcraftuk.com

A community interest company aiming to embed a 'Forest School' ethos into the educational framework in the south-east of England.

Embercombe

www.embercombe.org

A charity and social enterprise that runs experiential and leadership programmes for children, teenagers and adults. It aims to reconnect people to nature, community and themselves through transformative experiences.

LIFEbeat

www.lifebeat.co.uk

A charity providing transformational learning experiences for teenagers and adults through week-long summer camps for 14–18-year-olds, followed up with mentoring support and reunions. LIFEbeat's approach is based around the Creative Community Model originally created by Partners for Youth Empowerment in the US.

More on mindfulness

General:

Brach, Tara, *True Refuge: Finding Peace and Freedom in Your Own Awakened Heart*, London: Hay House, 2013

Chödrön, Pema, *When Things Fall Apart: Heart Advice for Difficult Times*, Shaftesbury, Dorset: Element Books, 2007

Heaversedge, Jonty, and Halliwell, Ed, *The Mindful Manifesto: How Doing Less and Noticing More Can Help Us Thrive In a Stressed-out World*, London: Hay House, 2012

Huber, Cheri, and Narayanan, Ashwini, *I Don't Want To, I Don't Feel Like It: How Resistance Controls Your Life and What to Do About It*, Murphys, Ca: Keep It Simple Books, 2013

Kabat-Zinn, Jon, *Full Catastrophe Living: How To Cope With Stress, Pain and Illness Using Mindfulness Meditation*, London: Piatkus, 1996

Nhat Hanh, Thich, *The Miracle of Mindfulness: The Classic Guide to Meditation by the World's Most Revered Master*, London: Rider, 1991

Wax, Ruby, *A Mindfulness Guide for the Frazzled*, London: Penguin Life, 2016

Williams, Mark, and Penman, Danny, *Mindfulness: A Practical Guide to Finding Peace in a Frantic World*, London: Piatkus, 2011

Williams, Mark, et al., *The Mindful Way Through Depression: Freeing Yourself from Chronic Unhappiness*, New York: Guilford Press, 2007

Helping children to learn mindfulness:

Hawn, Goldie, and Holden, Wendy, *10 Mindful Minutes: Giving Our Children – and Ourselves – the Skills to Reduce Stress and Anxiety for Healthier, Happier Lives*, London: Piatkus, 2012

Kaiser Greenland, Susan, *The Mindful Child: How to Help Your Kid Manage Stress and Become Happier, Kinder and More Compassionate*, New York: Atria, 2010

Kerr, Christiane, *Bedtime Meditations for Kids (Calm Kids)*, Borough Green: Diviniti Publishing, 2005

Snel, Eline, *Sitting Still Like a Frog: Mindfulness Exercises for Kids (and Their Parents)*, Boulder, CO: Shambhala Publications, 2014

Personal growth, parenting and neuroscience

Brown, Brené, *Daring Greatly: How the Courage to Be Vulnerable Transforms the Way We Live, Love, Parent, and Lead*, New York: Gotham Books, 2012

Faber, Adele, and Mazlish, Elaine, *How to Talk So Teens Will Listen and Listen So Teens Will Talk*, London: Piccadilly Press, 2006

Gilbert, Paul, *The Compassionate Mind (Compassion Focused Therapy)*, London: Constable, 2010

Hanson, Rick, *Buddha's Brain: The Practical Neuroscience of Happiness, Love and Wisdom*, Oakland, Ca: New Harbinger, 2009

Hughes, Daniel, and Baylin, Jonathan, *Brain-Based Parenting: The Neuroscience of Caregiving for Healthy Attachment*, New York: W.W. Norton, 2012

Jensen, Frances, *The Teenage Brain: A Neuroscientist's Survival Guide to Raising Adolescents and Young Adults*, London: Harper Thorson, 2015

Kabat-Zinn, Jon, and Kabat-Zinn, Myla, *Everyday Blessings: The Inner Work of Mindful Parenting*, London: Hachette Books, 1998

Kornfield, Jack, *A Path with Heart: A Guide Through the Perils and Promises of Spiritual Life*, London: Bantam, 1993

Levine, Amir, and Heller, Rachel, *Attached: Identify Your Attachment Style and Find Your Perfect Match*, London: Penguin, 2010

Morgan, Nicola, *Blame My Brain: The Amazing Teenage Brain Revealed*, London: Walker Books, updated edn 2013

Neff, Kristin, *Self Compassion: Stop Beating Yourself Up and Leave Insecurity Behind*, London: Yellow Kite, 2011

Neufeld, Gordon, and Maté, Gabor, *Hold Onto Your Kids: Why Parents Need to Matter More Than Peers*, New York: Ballantine Books, 2006

Parkin, John, C., *F*** It: The Ultimate Spiritual Way*, London: Hay House, 2014

Perry, Bruce, and Szalavitz, Maia, *Born for Love: Why Empathy Is Essential – and Endangered*, New York: William Morrow, 2010

Richo, David, *When Love Meets Fear: Becoming Defense-less and Resource-full*, Mahwah, NJ: Paulist Press, 1997

Senior, Jennifer, *All Joy and No Fun: The Paradox of Modern Parenthood*, London: Virago, 2015

Siegel, Daniel, and Hartzell, Mary, *Parenting from the Inside Out: How a Deeper Self-understanding Can Help You Raise Children Who Thrive*, New York: Jeremy P. Tarcher/Penguin, 2003

Siegel, Daniel, *Brainstorm: The Power and Purpose of the Teenage Brain*, New York: Jeremy P. Tarcher/Penguin, 2013

Stiffelman, Susan, *Parenting with Presence: Practices for Raising Conscious, Confident, Caring Kids* (Eckhart Tolle edn), Novato, CA: New World Library, 2015

Tolle, Eckhart, *A New Earth: Create a Better Life*, New York: Dutton/Penguin, 2005

Tolle, Eckhart, *The Power of Now: A Guide to Spiritual Enlightenment*, London: Yellow Kite, 2001

Recommended apps

Headspace: Guided meditation and mindfulness
www.headspace.com

Among the best-known and most popular mindfulness apps, Headspace was co-founded by mindfulness expert Andy Puddicombe to make meditation more accessible. It includes guided meditations suitable for all levels as well as specific content focused on creativity, decreasing stress and increasing happiness.

Available on iTunes and Google Play.

Smiling Mind: Guided meditation and mindfulness (free)
www.smilingmind.com.au

Created in Australia by psychologists and educators, Smiling Mind was originally designed to help children and young people de-stress and stay calm. There are tailored programmes for different age groups starting at 7–11.

Available on iTunes and Google Play.

Calm: Guided meditations and relaxation (free)
www.calm.com

This simple-to-use app aims to help you meditate, sleep or relax. It includes the 'Seven Steps of Calm', which is aimed at beginners and experienced meditators alike, as well as other guided sessions running from 2–30 minutes with a range of background scenes and nature sounds.

Available on iTunes and Google Play.

Mindfulness Bell (free)
Set it to ring a Tibetan singing bowl at intervals throughout the day to remind you to take a pause and check in with yourself.

Available on Google Play.

Insight Timer (free)
www.insighttimer.com

A meditation timer that doubles as a mindfulness guide and includes guided meditations by well-known teachers such as Eckhart Tolle, Thich Nhat Hanh, Tara Brach, Jack Kornfield, Jon Kabat-Zinn and others.

Available on iTunes and Google Play.

RESOURCES

Gratitude Journal – the original!
www.happytapper.com

A well-known gratitude journal founded by Carla White in 2008. You can add photos, tag Facebook friends, geotag your entries, and share what you're grateful for with loved ones.

Available on iTunes and Google Play.

Gratitude Garden (free)
www.izzymcrae.com/gratitude

This excellent, innovative app designed by Izzy McRae helps you maintain a gratitude practice by noting down three good things that have happened over the past 24 hours. As you progress, you receive points you can use to build a virtual 'garden'.

Available on iTunes and Google Play.

EasyPeasy
www.easypeasyapp.com

EasyPeasy supports learning through play at home, helping children develop the skills they need for school and beyond. Children develop key skills like concentration, creativity and determination through positive play and positive interactions with their parents.

Acknowledgements

This book is the fruit of all I have learned from the hundreds of families I've had the privilege of working with, and I would like to thank them for the trust they have placed in me during our sessions together and the many lessons they have taught me. Parents are building the foundations of all our tomorrows – and they are all heroes.

I owe everything in my life to my grandparents, Marguerite and Peter. The kindest, gentlest and most caring man I ever met, my granddad died at the age of eighty-eight, a few weeks before this book was completed. He and Nanny showed me all the love, patience and tenderness any child could have wished for. My granddad always encouraged me to follow my dreams and told me that anything was possible: and this book is proof he was right. I know my mum Amanda's influence has also flowed through these pages – and that she is still watching my progress from beyond the veil of everyday reality. I'd also like to thank the rest of my family, including Auntie Vivien, Paul, my cousin Josh, my cousin Alex and his wife Laura, and my Auntie June for all the love and support they provided while this book was being written.

I'd also like to thank those who showed me so much kindness when I was going through my own difficult times in childhood, including Julie and John Gilham, Rachael Fleming, Mary, John and Rebecca Wright and my godparents Graham and Margaret. I also owe a great debt to Charlotte Corbett, Margaret Norden, and all at the Central School of Dancing in Norwich.

A very special thank you to my wonderful partner, Matt, who has been there for me on this writing journey every step of the way, and who has turned every day into an adventure in love and laughter.

ACKNOWLEDGEMENTS

My friends have been an ever-ready source of insight, humour and encouragement, especially Kirsty Young, Katie Rogers, Katie Coldham, and Annette Sloly and her husband David. Many thanks also to Rose Latham, Sarah Chandler, Julie Damant, Catriona Metcalfe, Louise Taylor, Emma Sisley, Hannah Nedas, Nicola Gambin, Jane Bradbury, Ramona Burrage and Edward Walsh. Daniel Simpson, Katie Green, Justin Quirk and Kate Holt have also been unflagging and inspiring supporters of this project.

At the University of Kent, I'd like to thank Professors Derek Rutter and Lyn Quine, who supervised my masters in health psychology. I would not have been able to complete this course without the generous support of the Royal Pinner School Foundation, to whom I am eternally indebted. I am also extremely grateful for the incredible opportunity I had to train at Salomons, Canterbury Christ Church University, and to all the expert tutors and supervisors who taught me so much about psychology, and myself. A special thanks to Professor Paul Camic and Dr Louise Goodbody.

In more recent times, I've had the privilege of working with, and learning from, my many fantastic colleagues in the NHS, in private practice and in the public sector, who are too numerous to name but whose wisdom and skill has informed every one of these pages.

As a newcomer to publishing, I could not have asked for a more supportive and visionary team than my agent Claire Conrad of Janklow & Nesbit, my publisher Brenda Kimber and all at Transworld, and my television agent Jo Wander at Wander Management. Thank you for your patient guidance and the faith you have had in *Five Deep Breaths*.

Journal

Journal

Journal

Journal

Journal

Journal

Journal

Journal

Journal

Journal

Journal

Journal

Index

INDEX

INDEX

About the author

Dr Genevieve von Lob is a clinical psychologist who has worked with families from every type of background during a ten-year career spanning private practice, NHS Child and Adolescent Mental Health Services and work for local authorities. She has been widely quoted in the media, including in the *Telegraph, Financial Times, Top Santé* and *Grazia*, and featured as a consultant therapist in an episode of Channel 4's *Dispatches*. She lives in south-west London and enjoys playing the piano and singing in her spare time.

www.drvonlob.com